Politics & the Media:
Harlots and Prerogatives at the Turn
of the Millennium

Politics & the Media: Harlots and Prerogatives at the Turn of the Millennium

Edited by

Jean Seaton

Blackwell Publishers

Copyright © The Political Quarterly Publishing Co. Ltd.

ISBN 0–631–206191–1

First published 1998

Blackwell Publishers
108 Cowley Road, Oxford, OX1 1JF, UK.

and
350 Main Street,
Malden, MA 02148, USA.

British Library Cataloguing in Publication Data
A catalogue record for this book is available from the British Library

Library of Congress Cataloging in Publication Data
Cataloging-in-Publication data applied for

Printed in Great Britain by Whitstable Litho Ltd, Whitstable.

CONTENTS

Acknowledgements

The essays in this book were the product of a Political Quarterly Conference held at St Catherine's College, Oxford in September 1997. Those who took part in the conference were Steve Barnett, Eric Barendt, Audrey Coppard, James Cornford, Bernard Crick, James Curran, Simon Frith, Andrew Gamble, David Goodhart, Geoffrey Hodgson, David Jordan, John Lloyd, Michael Levy, Denis MacShane MP, Ben Pimlott, Peter Riddell, Martin Rowson, Philip Schlesinger, Jean Seaton, Colin Seymour-Ure, Tony Smith and Tony Wright MP

Introduction

JEAN SEATON

THIS book is about politics and what people think politics is. In particular, it is about how the mass media in Britain cover political life. It was put together at a key historical moment, on the basis of papers delivered a few months after the beginning of the first new government for eighteen years. In some ways, it seemed a hopeful time, indicating that the nation's democratic institutions were in working order, and able to respond to a change of political climate. Yet if—in one sense—it was a moment of triumph, it was also a time when political dependence on (even capitulation to) the media and media industries seemed to reach a new level. This partly reflected the reality of mass communications in flux: changes in the structure, markets, values, content and style of broadcasting, newspapers and the new information technology appeared to have affected traditional behaviour in politics in fundamental ways.

A key question has been choice. On the whole, media analysts have abandoned the standard arguments of the 'old' left in the 1970s and 1980s, which automatically equated the growth of big cartels and monopolies with a restriction of freedom. Far more common has been the opposite assumption, that rapid advances in technology and the expansion of global markets inevitably provide more choice. However, the issue remains: choice is not simply quantifiable. Choice of what, and for what ends? It is perfectly possible for choice to widen in a strictly numerical sense (for example, a proliferation of TV channels), and narrow in a qualitative one (a repetition of themes, dictated by advertising pressures, across the board).

In this book, academics, journalists and politicians with differing perspectives on the media attempt to make sense of the changes that have taken place, and their past and possible future impact. In particular, they tackle three problems that currently trouble the (in some respect) disturbingly calm waters of contemporary democratic politics. The first is whether the 'choice' on offer is actually excessive, fragmenting talent and resources into too many competing entertainments and discordant opportunities, and squeezing out serious discussion of the kind a healthy democracy requires. Thus, it may be argued, market pressures are trivialising what matters most to national life, and forcing politicians to become, in a variety of ways, part of the entertainment business: that is part of the meaning of 'spin'. The second is whether it is simply naive, under such conditions, to expect journalists to be serious in ways that politicians are ceasing to be, given the market pressures that are isolating those with serious ideas, independent knowledge, or specialist interests. The third is the shift in the location of the political arena: the

Published by Blackwell Publishers, 108 Cowley Road, Oxford OX4 1JF, UK and 350 Main Street, Malden, MA 02148, USA

extent to which the media, which claim to describe or reflect what is going on in democratic politics, have actually become the main political theatre, brokering the most important events and staging the most important exchanges.

There are a number of ways in which these issues can be approached. Thus, Andrew Graham, from an economist's perspective, is an enthusiastic believer in the potential political and social value of the technology, but shows how crude much of the thinking on the topic has so far been. In particular, he challenges the conventional wisdom on the capacity of digital technology to improve variety of news coverage and comment. He describes, in particular, the likely consequences of the growing trend towards cross media ownership, pointing to evidence that all media industries are becoming increasingly monopolistic. Although there are more television channels, he argues, they are owned by ever-more powerful companies which dominate the entire production process. He dismisses the view that the 'products' of the mass media—entertainment, news and opinion—should be treated in exactly the same way as any other commodity: in a democracy, he suggests, non-market-led innovation in ideas plays a vital role.

Graham's essay relates directly to the theme of the centrality of the media to the institutional structure. Peter Riddell looks directly at the most important democratic institution of all. Examining the relationship between Parliament and the media, Riddell sees a leakage of power from the Commons to quangos and regulatory bodies, and a failure by the media to keep pace with the change, leaving huge areas of effective government unaccountable, unscrutinised and unchallenged. Riddell points to the way in which Parliament has come to be used by politicians, especially ministers, as little more than a media opportunity; yet also at the way that pressures on politicians work on journalists as well. News, for example, is increasingly seen as expensive, unappealing to the young and hence to advertisers, and consequently not always worth the money in commercial terms. Moreover, under such conditions, 'news value' has a different meaning: the rapid working of the new technology means that many stories are born, die, and are replaced so fast, that it is scarcely worth covering them except in a cursory way.

Tony Wright wryly explores the underbelly of Riddell's argument. How, he asks, do politicians carve out careers—of a necessarily different kind—in the changed environment? He turns the 'decline of Parliament' argument around: Parliament can only retain old functions and acquire new ones if it reforms; but it needs media cooperation to do so. The media, however, can scarcely be expected to help spontaneously. Paradoxically, they would certainly be encouraged by a more elevated, less media-oriented political debate: a point stressed in a later chapter, in which the editor re-examines the myths that have grown up around the liberal concept of freedom of speech which, in the classic literature, entailed the obligation to use freedom constructively. Thus, nineteenth-century writers presented democracy not as a battlefield, but as an organic and creative debate.

Some of the problems identified defy solutions. One of these is the new problem of being observed: an aspect of technology that has crept up on the modern citizen. In William Faulkner's novel, *The Light in August*, the dying hero, Christmas, looks up at his executioners 'with his eyes open and empty of everything except consciousness . . . for a long moment he looked at them with peaceful and unfathomable and unbearable eye'.[1] Looking transformed into being seen. A modern politician is like Christmas: and his modern craft is not so much the art of the possible, as the art of appearing to be possible. The language of politics is, of course, saturated with the notion of being seen: image, reflection, transparency, obscurity, clarity, are all words that crop up time and again. Physical appearance has always mattered: as the Romans were aware, when they identified the virtues and power of the state by placing stylised portraits of the emperor on coins. But how we interpret the visual symptoms of good government is far less certain. Modern media have simply added their contribution. In particular, television—with its organised, partial and deceptively 'honest' eye—has been the most powerful pressure on the politics of appearances, so that the power of the political speech directed at a few thousand has been replaced by the power of the make-up artist, the tailor and the manicurist. In some ways the power is greater. But a visual impression is not susceptible to dialogue or argument. Moreover, the visual as opposed to the spoken statement is not simply about the physiognomy of politicians. Much political discourse has been replaced by spectacle: where nineteenth-century citizens listened or read Gladstone's thunderous imprecations about Armenian massacres, the modern public watches the silent reproaches of children in Bosnia or Rwanda.

How do we judge what we see, as opposed to what we hear? The process is fraught with dark emotions, and always has been. Orpheus loved Eurydice, yet condemned her to the underworld with a hungrily adoring look. Narcissus was driven to suicide by a fixated love for his own reflection. To gaze at Medusa was to meet instant death, while the sight of the sirens was so strong a magnet that Odysseus had himself tethered to the mast in order to enjoy the pleasure of seeing, while escaping their fatal enticement. It is not surprising, therefore, that the living-room gaze of a politician—or film star, or princess—should be capable of an hypnotic effect, in some cases, and of irritation or revulsion in others. Nor should it be remarkable that the omnipresent modern media, with their ability to project negative as well as positive images, can have such a destructive force.

Part of that force depends on mass sadism, and the media's willingness to incite it. 'The sense of satisfaction which the public can obtain from the humiliation of prominent people', as the BBC's Nick Jones observed, during the Major administration, as minister after minister was exposed for one kind of transgression or another, 'and the perverse pleasure which journalists can sometimes derive from collusion in destroying those whom they may have helped achieve prominence in the first place, is perhaps the least discussed new phenomenon'.[2] The trend is certainly unmistakable: towards personalised politics, often aided by a visual element. In the end, it is often the visual impact that saves a Norris, and fells a Mellor, on such occasions.

The importance of visual news—almost to the exclusion of any other kind—was dramatically demonstrated in the aftermath of the death of Diana, Princess of Wales in August 1997. Diana's own complicity with the media—her part-reluctant, part-teasing acceptance of an institutionalised, yet informal stardom—helped in her lifetime to make her (as was frequently said) the best-known woman in the world, a status that seemed to be enhanced rather than diminished by the infrequency with which she was ever heard actually to speak. Her life was played out in images—some stolen and voyeuristic, others freely, even manipulatively, given—of triumph and exploitation, which left the public tantalisingly unsure whether to see her as a powerful media goddess or a hapless victim.

After her death, the visual aspect was enhanced: so much so, that it was as if she was indeed immortal. More newspapers were sold, more space in them was devoted to photographs, more hours per person per day of television were watched, than ever before in history. There were arguments after the tragedy, about the Monarchy, its role and future. Yet, significantly, they focused on the visual symbolism, more than any words: the failure to fly a flag at half-mast, the Queen's bow to the passing cortege, the Kensington Gardens floral shrine, the silent weeping people in the street. The semi-hysteria of the moment revealed an extraordinary public emotion that was undeniably genuine, yet also one that derived from long-standing media impressions, an aspect developed by Ben Pimlott in his historical examination of the Monarchy-media nexus. Pimlott shows how a healthily democratic decline in deference brought a dangerous, profit-driven populism in its wake. In doing so, he delivers a sharp warning to all political institutions (and leaders) who become too media-dependent.

The politically-focused media eye can be merciless. It can also, of course, be surgical. Modern elections have increasingly become visual events, designed as theatre specifically for television: none more so than the last, in which (according to one study), the average length of a politician's news-broadcast soundbite was squeezed to less than ten seconds.[3] When the polls closed there was a rare episode of fact and science, as the results poured in and were subject to statistical analysis. Yet one of the highpoints of an extraordinary election night was a split-second moment of purely visual drama: as an ashen Michael Portillo accepted his defeat at the hands of Stephen Twigg, whose face described the mood of disbelief, and of wildest dreams come true, that characterised the night. The effect was heightened by cuts to other Conservative leaders—Gillian Shepherd, and especially John Major—who were experiencing their own personal dramas. Thus, in a short span, the story was composed by the roving camera (or, rather, by the team that directed its shots) for the benefit of the nation, with few words of any significance being spoken.

The camera does not lie—but it interprets. So does the potentially savage eye of the political cartoonist, the demand for whose art—despite the immediacy of the electronic media—shows no sign of diminishing. Cartoons amuse by encapsulating reality through graphic metaphor and distortion that writers have difficulty in putting into words. The joke comes from the splinter of truth. In his cartoon in this volume, Martin Rowson pins down a political atmosphere, in a way that is not unrelated to the actual-but-edited reality of the Portillo-Twigg shots.

If visual effects have become the message, it is natural that politicians should spend more time on self-presentation, bringing it into the heart of the policy-making process, as—in complementary ways—the Freedom of Information White Paper and the official report on the Government Information Service (setting out to 'improve co-ordination with and from the centre, so as to get across consistently the Government's key policies and themes'[4]) both make clear. Yet politicians and their concerns are only part of the equation. What determines the nature and behaviour of the media much more than political steers or even legislation, is the commercial marketplace, and the status of media organisations as profit-seeking, or at least breaking-even, businesses. The growth of conglomerates, and its policy consequences, is a key theme of this book. If newspapers have fallen victim to a ruthless pricing war that threatens to destroy genuine journalistic competition, then in broadcasting powerful lobbying by vested interests in favour of a commercial union of telephone and broadcasting delivery systems, and against regulation, has been one of the most frightening demonstrations of the ruthlessness of the very media that regulation might conceivably restrain.

One consequence of cross-media competition, as opposed to monopoly, it has frequently been argued in the past, is to 'tabloidise' the media. Television has responded to the increasing tendency of popular papers to rely on pictures rather than print, by taking a more tabloid news agenda, while the press, in turn, has been reacting to an earlier fear of the immediacy of television images. The process has partly been a matter of reducing intellectual—or any other kind—of serious content: it has partly been about tailoring content to the advertising marketplace. But whatever the cause, the effect, it has been suggested, has been a merging of style and content of print journalism and broadcasting, including a recent and alarming process of 'dumbing-down' the quality newspapers in a tabloid direction, adopting popular-press layout, style and visual effects. Meanwhile, television stations—formerly spread across a spectrum of seriousness—have become less and less differentiated. In his chapter, Steven Barnett examines these arguments. In particular, he looks at the nature and methods of down-marketing—raising the question of whether any remaining viewers or readers are to be found lower down the educational scale, and whether the only available, and unfilled, niche is higher up: contrary to the red-neck assumptions of the trade, better, more intelligent journalism would have a competitive edge.

Some of the alterations in the media/politics relationship reflect systemic changes in the political world. One of the most historic has been the decision to proceed with Welsh and, especially, Scottish devolution. In his chapter,

Philip Schlesinger assesses the extent to which growing European integration, on the one hand, and the establishment of a Scottish Assembly with independent powers on the other, will affect the political culture, especially as viewed through, and partially shaped by, an already established national Scottish media.

Will Scottish media, focusing more than ever on Scottish affairs, help to create a political micro-climate, in which nationally-oriented parties can flourish? Will they be more balanced than their UK equivalents, or less? Part of the answer depends on the future of media impartiality, or at any rate independence, in Britain as a whole, and on the future of the right to freedom of speech, linked to the freedom to reach a large, appropriate audience. The issue is key to democracy: by protecting an opponent's right to be heard, a democratic politician secures his or her own voice in opposition. The point has long been understood, but better so in broadcasting than in newspapers: but it has not always been acted upon. As Eric Barendt points out, many of the traditional assumptions about the buttressing of impartiality or 'balance' in broadcasting no longer operate. His suggested remedy is recourse to the courts, which have historically been hesitant to interfere in the media, but ought now, he maintains, be encouraged to do so, to reinforce the gentlemen's understandings and conventions that have underpinned broadcast journalism, but which have recently broken down, and are likely to do so even more in the new, multi-channelled environment.

Balance is one thing: opinion leadership is another. In the past, there was a clear division: broadcasting, both radio and television, strove because of official and unofficial guidelines to represent both sides of every party-political argument, while newspapers were systematically biased, mainly in a Tory direction. Colin Seymour-Ure notes the extent to which 1997 altered the pattern: both because of a (possibly temporary) shift of allegiance by several papers towards 'New' Labour, but also because of a crumbling of the concept of newspaper allegiance itself: so that all the broadsheets presented, and prided themselves on presenting, a cacophony of competing political opinions. Seymour-Ure points to the dangers, as well as advantages, of a rudderless press and a fluid electorate, lacking the old certainties of partisan ports of call.

Thus, the picture of the media industries overall appears to be one that combines increasing diversity with growing unity; competition with monopoly; influence with irrationality. It is a work environment that is ever more pressurised, and less respectful of journalists' own interests, concerns or knowledge; less concerned with accuracy, depth or seriousness of content. Yet it is also one that offers large numbers of people an enhanced opportunity to make their voices heard, as outlets proliferate, and every computer-owner becomes, in effect, a media proprietor. As this book shows, it is a time not just of tumultuous change in the media, but of excitement among political journalists, who feel, tangibly, the effects of a new administration. Will New Labour come as fiercely into conflict with the press as Old, during the Wilson and Callaghan governments, or Thatcher's and Major's? That intriguing question must be the subject of another volume.

Notes

1 William Faulkner, *The Light in August*, Harmondsworth, Penguin, 1987, p. 217.
2 Nick Jones, *Sound Bites and Spin Doctors*, London, Cassell, 1995, p. 63.
3 J. Harrison, 'Politics on Air', in David Butler and Denis Kavanagh, eds., *The British General Election of 1997*, Basingstoke, Macmillan, 1997, p. 142.
4 Report of the Working Group on the Government Information Service, Cabinet Office, November 1997, para 84. Also see *Your Right to Know: Freedom of Information*, Cm 3818, 1997.

Members and Millbank: the Media and Parliament

PETER RIDDELL

THE media have largely turned their back on Parliament, but then so have most leading politicians. For ambitious MPs, membership of the House of Commons is a necessary route to influence and power and rather than any longer the centre of political debate. Becoming an MP is a necessary pre-condition for belonging to the closed shop of career politicians, and, as such, the crucial first step on the promotion ladder to a ministerial office or a shadow post. Politicians who lose their seats soon find out how uninteresting they are to the media, unless they are suspected of having ambitions to return to the Commons, like Michael Portillo. However, activities in Parliament itself, speeches and questions, are seldom central either to long-term promotion or to the main political decisions.

The main arena of political debate is now the broadcasting studio, not the floor of the Commons. This trend has been accentuated by the arrival of the Blair Government. New Labour has shown little interest in the Commons, either in Opposition or since winning the 1997 election. Tony Blair would rather spend his evenings at home with his family in his Downing Street flat than chatting with parliamentary colleagues at the Commons while waiting to vote (which he does not do very often in any case). The Labour leadership and whips regard the vast army of backbenchers as a problem to be managed, and preferably to be kept away from the media—for instance, via constituency weeks when new MPs are sent away from Westminster.

New Labour strategists have regarded appearances by Mr Blair and other ministers in the Commons as merely one part of a communications strategy rather than a central aspect of democratic accountability. New policies have often been launched at specially arranged media events and photo-opportunities—on rundown housing estates, schools or hospitals—before anything formal is said in the Commons. Over the first long session of the new Parliament, Betty Boothroyd, the Commons Speaker, regularly made known her annoyance to senior ministers that important policy statements were first becoming known through newspaper and broadcasting leaks which had obviously originated with them and their advisers.

For many senior MPs, and those that retired at the 1992 and 1997 elections, this shift of attention away from the Commons is one of the most significant, and regrettable, changes of the past generation—and it is often accompanied by complaints about the disappearance from the broadsheet papers of extensive reporting of speeches on the floor of the House. But concentrating on the end of gallery coverage misses the point, and ignores the broader, and most important, changes in the past decade in the behaviour of politicians, as well as in the character of the media. There is plenty to worry about in the media's coverage politics—the tendency to focus on scandal and splits rather than policy and process, the increasingly partisan and committed nature of much political reporting and the rise of the celebrity journalists. But the reduction in reporting of what is said on the floor of the Commons itself is not the most important issue.

Decline of the Commons Chamber

Politicians and media have both adjusted their behaviour so that the proceedings in the Commons are now just one, subsidiary, feature of political coverage. Television has become the main direct medium for political leaders to communicate with the public and speaking in the Commons is merely one means of doing do, and by no means the most satisfactory one for politicians eager to define the terms on which they appear against a friendly rather than confrontational background.

On big days when an important story is breaking, the Commons chamber is often deserted, apart from MPs waiting impatiently to speak. Even the members' lobby just outside the chamber, the rialto for gossip between MPs and journalists, can be fairly empty, at least of these in the know. Instead, assiduous journalists will wander across the road to College Green (sound bite heaven), or a couple of hundred yards to four Millbank, the home of the BBC, ITN and Sky studios. Ministers and their shadows will be found there in a round of interviews. Similarly, when a major policy initiative is to be launched, it will invariably have been leaked/previewed in that morning's newspapers. The relevant minister will have appeared on the Today programme on Radio Four. It is hardly surprising therefore that, apart from the annual Budget and rare speeches by the Prime Minister, the Commons chamber is usually sparsely attended for ministerial statements about the details of new proposals.

When a newly elected MP asked me after the 1997 general election whether anything he said in the chamber would be reported, I said no. He would only attract media attention by his activities outside the chamber, writing pamphlets for think tanks and articles in the press, or participating in broadcasts. Speeches and interventions on the floor of the Commons are basically aimed at parliamentary colleagues, and particularly party whips. Commons performances are to show that the MP is a sound, hard-working chap willing to support the frontbench, who therefore deserves favour and promotion. A solid record in the chamber is necessary to impress other MPs, not to achieve public prominence or build up his or her overall political reputation. But since the first steps on the ladder of promotion are usually thanks to the whips, such activity in the chamber is still necessary, even if it is largely ignored by the press and the broadcasters. Solid performances on the floor of the Commons were a crucial first step in securing the early promotion to the frontbench of Tony Blair and Gordon Brown, but, at most, only partially explains their subsequent rise to prominence and power.

This is a world away from the traditional newspaper dominated coverage of politics focused on the floor of the House of Commons. All important political initiatives used to be announced in the Commons. MPs attended the wind-up speeches closing debates between 9 and 10 in the evening, knowing that they would be able to read about the exchanges and much else that had occurred in the House in lengthy reports in the next morning's papers.

Moreover, until just over forty years ago, there was a formal rule banning the discussion of issues on radio and television due to come before either chamber over the following fortnight. The fourteen day rule, a wartime invention, was vigorously defended in the early 1950s by both Churchill and Attlee. Sir Winston Churchill complained just before his departure from 10 Downing Street in 1955 that 'it would be shocking to have debates in this House forestalled, time after time, by expressions of opinion by persons who had not the status or responsibility of MPs . . . on this new robot organisation of television and BBC broadcasting'. These restrictions did not, however, long survive the departure of Churchill and Attlee: it collapsed during the Suez crisis. The cautious, deferential approach to politics of the BBC was challenged by the arrival of independent television and radical, brash young reporters like Robin Day.

Rise of Television

Television has been the driving force of the changing relationship between the media and Parliament. The steady growth of current affairs programmes on television and on radio since the late 1950s has provided a more direct way for leading politicians to communicate with the public. News is now a continuous 24 hour a day phenomenon, rather than determined by the deadlines of evening and morning papers. Politicians have responded. What is said on the *Today* Programme often dominates the early editions of the *Evening Standard*, and is then taken up on the lunchtime bulletins, all before the Commons has started sitting for the day. Terms like soundbite, instant or rapid rebuttal, news cycle and the ludicrous spin doctor (who have neither the subtlety of spin bowlers nor the professionalism of doctors) became part of the jargon of the media and of the grandly titled communications directors, previously called press secretaries. The latter used to behave more like superior servants, gentlemen's gentlemen like Sir Harold Evans, who served Harold Macmillan and Alec Home, rather than the virtual equals of ministers that their successors have become.

The parties know they have a better chance of influencing the political agenda by launching initiatives outside the Commons, rather than inside the House, where the other party or parties have a right of reply. For instance, all Gordon Brown's main policy proposals in Opposition were made outside the Commons, usually carefully leaked just before the formal announcement to one or two favoured journalists to stimulate interest among the broadcasters. Mr Brown's exchanges in the Commons with Kenneth Clarke were usually knockabout: entertaining to the couple of dozen MPs attending, diverting to the parliamentary sketch-writers, but otherwise ignored by both the broadcasters and the newspapers. Labour has behaved in largely the same say in Government, with rare exceptions. Mr Blair is far more likely to give a radio or television interview or to appear on the pages of a tabloid or broadsheet paper with an article written by him, or in his name, than he is likely to speak in the Commons.

The arrival of television cameras in the House of Commons in 1989 has not reversed this shift away from the Chamber. Indeed, the most important result has been the creation of the extensive broadcasting studios in Four Millbank which has made it easier for the BBC, ITV and Sky to interview politicians at Westminster. Such studio, or outside, interviews and the 'talking head' comments of correspondents, are usually a much larger proportion of news reports than what is said on the floor of the Commons. Direct, and particularly live, coverage is dominated by Prime Minister's Questions (after May 1997, once rather than twice a week). On the main evening bulletins, a short clip from PM's questions is usually the only direct reference to anything that has happened in Parliament and it normally features as just one part of a report covering all aspects of an issue, alongside the views of others affected. This is an understandable news judgment. The main party leaders and their offices spend a lot of time carefully preparing soundbites in order to have a short clip shown on the early and main evening news bulletins. Whether such soundbites are broadcast is regarded as the main yardstick of success for the parties, much more than the immediate impact of the exchanges in the House itself upon MPs attending.

Television has added to the pressure to change some of the arcane procedures of the House: for instance, cutting some of the jargon. Leading politicians are now aware that they are addressing the public as well as fellow MPs. It is no coincidence that Budget speeches have been shorter in the 1990s than before the arrival of cameras, or even the start of sound broadcasting in the late 1970s. Television has also occasionally shown Select Committee hearings when someone at the centre of a controversy is being questioned by MPs. The cameras may therefore have increased interest in Parliament, though there is no evidence that they have increased respect for Parliament: the reverse, given the frequent criticism of PM's questions.

Decline of Newspaper Coverage

The fragmentation of political news, away from the Chamber into broadcasting studios, news conferences and select committees, has been reflected in the press. This has been most vividly reflected in the disappearance of gallery coverage. In 1992, Jack Straw organised a study of the quantity of press reporting of Parliament over a sixty-year period. This showed that reporting of what has been said on the floor of the Commons, in broadsheet papers, had dropped very sharply. In *The Times*, the daily coverage of Parliament varied between 40 and 1,050 lines between the early 1930s and late 1980s. But, by the year of the study, fewer than 100 lines a day were dedicated to the proceedings of Parliament, and since then the total has dropped even further. Mr Straw complained that, 'the decline in press coverage of Parliament must have a serious affect on the public's understanding of our democratic system'.

The decline in traditional direct reporting began in the 1980s. As Political Editor of the *Financial Times* between 1981 and 1988, I played a role in the change by ending the traditional distinction between gallery coverage and lobby stories which provide background and descriptions of activities outside the Chamber. Frequently, reports on speeches or exchanges in the Chamber form just a few paragraphs or sentences within a broader political story, also including remarks broadcast on television, a lobby (that is non-attributable) comment by a minister or backbencher (invariably though often inaccurately described as 'senior') together with interpretation of the implications. On the FT's Parliament and Politics page in this period, there was usually a mix of such stories plus one or two more traditional gallery reports. But the decline of gallery coverage was symbolised when *The Times* scrapped its full politics page in 1990.

The shift of balance was, and is, justified by the shift of focus of political debates that I have described earlier. It reflects the impact of television, the relative unimportance and predictability of the Chamber during Lady Thatcher's heyday in the 1980s and, again now, given the size of Labour's majority, and a change of generations both amongst political editors and politicians. The old cosy club involving a couple of dozen middle-aged male lobby journalists and politicians is now long over. The press gallery, and it is increasingly also a broadcasters' gallery, is now younger, less stuffy and more female. There have been gains for readers and viewers: a less deferential and secretive attitude, fuller coverage of select committees and behind-the-scenes manoeuvres, both in Whitehall and in Westminster, and a more open political debate. Also it is wrong to be starry-eyed about the political reporting of the past: the longer stories of that era often simply amounted to a regurgitated and dull official line of the day masked under phrases such as 'authoritative sources' and the like. Responding to Jack Straw's analysis in 1993, I wrote that the public 'now know more of what is going on as the result of the assiduous work by reporters in the lobbies than would ever have been gleaned by sitting in the press gallery'. I am now much less sanguine.

Moving Down-market

There has not only been a shift of emphasis, a rebalancing of coverage to match the changed behaviour of politicians and the media. Quality has also suffered in all the main broadsheet papers. This reflects the impact of the newspaper price war and increased competition which has put a premium on items that are believed to attract new and younger readers who are seen as less interested in politics, at least conventional Westminster politics. Detailed political coverage is low on that list. It is regarded as boring by a new and brasher generation of newspaper executives. The amount of space devoted to politics in all its forms has declined, and there has been a shift of emphasis towards more personality based stories. The press has become much more intrusive into the private lives of politicians.

The news, and features, though not the opinion, pages of all the main broadsheets have changed. There have been moves downmarket with the 'Daily Mailisation' of news and night desks. Bob Franklin of Sheffield University has become an obituarist of the traditional Press Gallery. He has noted in *Parliamentary Affairs* (April 1996) an increasing emphasis on scandal and misconduct rather than on policy issues such as health, education or law and order and, I would add, questions of procedure and structure. The 'backbench' on newspapers that decides which stories appear, and their presentation, prefers scandal and personalities to analysis and policy, though the latter can still appear on big occasions. The outrageous is more likely to be reported than the significant if it is less newsworthy in conventional terms. Publicity-conscious MPs know that to attract coverage they need to include catchy soundbites in press releases or in broadcast interviews.

Bob Franklin has highlighted other trends: a growing preoccupation with the activities of government and senior politicians to the relative neglect of backbenchers and minority parties (the Liberal Democrats have constantly had to struggle for coverage except when they win by-elections); and an increasingly critical tone, 'more polarised, less measured and less willing to be neutral in its appraisals of parliamentary affairs'.

The increasing importance of television has had costs as well. The snappy and catchy are preferred over the reflective and considered. Pictures are better than words: personalities than policies. Rows, scandals and crises are more likely to attract attention than analyses, difference of nuance and changes in procedures. Politicians and their media advisers have become skilled at conveying their messages in ways appealing to the broadcasters. Inevitably the more deliberative way that Parliament functions is less glamorous, less newsworthy. Broadcasters point to the range of special political programmes, both covering Select Committees and designed for specific regions of the country. But these are put out at times when audiences are almost certain to be small. The changes in BBC Radio Four schedules that took effect in Spring 1998 not only demoted *Yesterday in Parliament* to long-wave, but also shifted the long-running *Week in Westminster* from its Saturday morning slot to Thursday evening. This cut its audience by two-thirds and also changed its character away from being a reflective programme covering a whole week, which has allowed backbenchers to air their views.

As a result, political coverage in the media is much less comprehensive than before. This is about much more than just the decline in direct gallery reporting of what is said in the Chamber, with which MPs are perhaps understandably concerned. The real question is whether the overall quality of reporting has declined, whether the public knows as much as it should about what is happening in politics. Admittedly, analysis of political trends and of detailed policy is better than twenty or thirty years ago, at least in the broadsheets. This is in part because of the growing prominence of specialist correspondents. The debate within Government on key issues, like Europe, is more fully reported. Very big parliamentary stories are still occasionally covered reasonably well in the broadsheets and on the main current affairs programmes, even if accounts of what is said in the House are only a minor part of reports. On a few important occasions, when there is a big vote or an important subject is being debated, *The Times* still offers a traditional gallery story of several hundred words, though it comes as often from the Lords as from the Commons.

However, the coverage in most papers lacks depth and context, as well as being squeezed in size. Personality differences are exaggerated, every dispute becomes a split, every small shift in position becomes a humiliating climb-down. Stories about policy developments, procedural changes and parliamentary reform, the activities of backbench groups, the work of think tanks, and new initiatives from backbenchers seldom appear. There is little consistency or follow-up. Readers may be told about a story for the few days when it is big news in conventional terms—a row, a scandal or a possible ministerial resignation. But they are seldom told what happened afterwards. The attention span of newspaper executives seems seldom to be more than a few days, or at least that is how they believe that their younger target readers will remain interested.

But the media are not solely to blame. The attention of the public, and MPs themselves, has moved away from the Chamber. Parliament itself has seemed less important in relation to other sources of power: a more active and assertive judiciary, utility regulators who can decide the future of large industries, European institutions, the pressures of the markets and everything summed up by the term globalisation. The Blair Government is in the process of creating alternative sources of power, and hence news, in the form of the Scottish Parliament and Welsh Assembly in 2000 with an elected mayor and assembly for London following shortly afterwards. These bodies will all challenge the traditional desire of Westminster virtually to monopolise political news. The Scottish press has already partly shifted its focus from Westminster to the new Edinburgh Parliament. In this respect the media are following rather than setting trends, recognising and reporting on where the real power lies.

The parties have also changed their approaches. Their media strategists are less concerned with the Commons. For them, what happens in the Palace of Westminster is now just one part of the permanent campaign, another source of soundbites. There is a danger of exaggerating the influence of such media strategies. The main parties are more skilful at trying to influence media, but journalists are not merely passive and uncritical recipients of news. They can, and do seek alternative views and interpretations. Part of the fun of being a political journalist is the multiplicity of sources within Westminster. Not only are the Opposition parties always eager to present their alternative to the view of the Government, but any minister, including the Prime Minister, has rivals on his or her own side who are eager to put over their own opinions.

Special and media advisers to ministers have become adept in creating a sense of dependency by promising a preview of a future event or initiative, or an 'exclusive' interview to favoured reporters or papers which do not rock the boat. This has been particularly true of the leading Blairite advisers such as Alastair Campbell, Tony Blair's main press spokesman and Charlie Whelan, Gordon Brown's personal spokesman. Political reporters, and news desks, are always frightened of not having covered a story, however minor. This is reinforced by the physical proximity of the main political reporters working in the same corridors in the crowded Press Gallery. Competition can produce sameness rather than diversity. The night logs of the newspapers are in general exercises in protecting the backs of those concerned, so that one paper always 'matches' stories of its rivals in later editions.

The changes in the media coverage of Parliament are part of a general shift in the coverage of politics. The balance sheet is not all on the debit side. American journalists visiting Britain during the 1997 election commented upon the seriousness of the daily press conferences when questions were asked about real policy issues, rather than merely opinion polls or campaign rows. Nonetheless, there are parallel complaints in the United States in the decline and quantity and quality in the coverage of Congress. There has been a similar increase in concentration on scandal and personalities. In part, these also reflect commercial pressures form new corporate owners, changing technologies and softer definitions of news to appeal to new, and younger, readers.

More Partisan

In Britain, the press has also become more partisan. Of course, newspapers have often taken sides in the party battle. In the 19th century and the early decades of this century, a number of the multitude of daily and evening papers were directly subsidised by the parties. The press barons of the first half of this century, notably Northcliffe, Rothermere, Beaverbrook and the Berry family, sought to exercise direct political influences. Their campaigns were often ineffective and expensive, testimony more to their vanity than their influence. The post-war generation of proprietors have—with a few exceptions like Robert Maxwell—mainly been more concerned with profit and loss accounts than with political power, except where their own commercial interests have been directly affected.

Nonetheless, these proprietors and the editors of mass-selling tabloids have been flattered by political leaders and media advisers to believe they have influence and can decide elections. I do not believe the press is really decisive. Even best-selling tabloids reinforce rather than create opinions. In deciding to back Labour and Tony Blair on the eve of the 1997 election campaign, the *Sun* followed an existing shift in the voting preferences of its readers in that direction over the preceding few years. Mr Blair and his advisers have assiduously courted the proprietors and editors of the main tabloids, and, even after Labour's landslide victory on 1 May 1997, they were extremely wary of confronting the strongly Euro-sceptic views of Rupert Murdoch and his editors.

A more significant shift has been in the character of press partisanship. Papers and journalists have not been content to analyse or even advocate. They have sought to be part of the political process. This has been shown vividly by the rise of Euro-sceptics to influence within the Tory party during the late 1980s and 1990s. This trend was aided by the rising influence and prominence of a group of sceptic journalists on the *Daily* and *Sunday Telegraph* and the *Daily Mail*, as well as the various News International titles, such as Charles Moore, Boris Johnson and Simon Heffer. But many papers are not monolithic and allow the occasional pro-European voice among the sceptic chorus. This sceptic shift has had a significant impact on the debate within the Tory party. There is the risk that prejudices, and hopes, of sceptic editors distort news coverage, as occurred during the Tory leadership contest of summer 1995. Not only were almost all Tory-supporting papers extremely hostile to John Major, but their front page news stories tended to write off his chances. There were tendentious, and in the event inaccurate, estimates of the 'danger' level of votes against him.

Hybrid Political Journalists

Moreover, the career paths of journalists and politicians have become increasingly blurred, both in Britain and in the United States. There have always been a number of journalists who have decided in their late 30s and 40s to become members of the House of Commons, notably Nigel Lawson, who excelled at both. But there are an increasing number of hybrid journalist-politicians who combine working for newspapers with active involvement in politics. This does not matter if they are not writing about politics and policy. But many do. Three leading journalists who wrote about political issues were recruited to work in Downing Street during Mr Blair's first year in office, admittedly all known Labour supporters. Of course, journalists cannot be political eunuchs. They have strong views, likes and dislikes. But a partisan commitment, such as being active in a party, inevitably creates obligations and can prevent a journalist being detached and critical when necessary. Alastair Campbell made no secret of his commitment, and close links with Neil Kinnock, before he became Mr Blair's press secretary in autumn 1994. But in other cases the commitment may be hidden and insidious with the journalist using his position to argue for a particular faction within a party and against another. A linked trend has been the rise of the highly paid celebrity journalist, both the household name anchors or correspondents of television programmes, and newspaper pundits who appear on the main talk shows. It is a long time since many were involved in direct, daily reporting and their financial and social positions are very different from their readers. Leading journalists increasingly share the educational and social backgrounds of the politicians they cover. They treat each other as equals, in marked contrast with the era before the 1970s when, as Sir Peregrine Worsthorne often likes to remind us, senior politicians regarded the press as social, and intellectual, inferiors. The change produces the risk of arrogance, of journalists thinking they are more important than politicians, and hence of presuming to determine what is rightfully the province of elected politicians.

The coverage of politics, and especially of Parliament, is therefore skewed and inadequate. I do not believe in some idealistic version of civic journalism. The media should not preach, and journalists should not become advocates of particular policies and interest groups (as some environmental correspondents often appear to be). What is needed is a sense of detachment and perspective, of what is significant rather than sensational. Current trends in reporting are worrying for the functioning of our democracy. There is too often a failure to distinguish between the public and the private. Private indiscretions that were not publicised in the past are now regarded as the public property of the media. Greater transparency on the operations of government and the financial affairs of politicians and political parties is desirable. But the tabloids are usually more interested in opening up entirely private matters.

This is not an argument for a return to the old club like secretive world of political journalists, let alone to the days of extensive gallery coverage of what is said on the floor of the House. Power and influence have moved elsewhere. Politics is more diverse. But that also imposes a duty on the press more fully to report these new centres of power: to explain, for example, what the judges, the utility regulators and the Monetary Policy Committee of the Bank of England do. We need more, as well as better balanced, political coverage than now, principally on these new wielders of power.

The media should report and analyse what is done by politicians on our behalf, to let readers and viewers know how we are governed. They are elected, and we are not. But this is not a blanket obligation. The media has to interest and retain the attention of its readers, listeners and viewers in an increasingly competitive media market. Parliament has to justify that it is worth reporting, not just that its procedures are comprehensible, but that what happens in the Palace of Westminster in itself matters. MPs have to show that they are not just engaged in an empty partisan ritual, but, rather, that they are holding ministers to account and scrutinising legislation properly. They have to show that the programme of reform launched in 1997 will make Parliament more effective, a place where political influence is exercised, rather than just where votes are counted. They have to show they deserve more extensive coverage. But the media in its turn needs to take politics more seriously.

Biographical Note

Peter Riddell is political columnist and Assistant Editor (Politics) on *The Times*. He has written a number of books about politics and most recently published *Parliament Under Pressure*, Gollancz, January 1998.

Inside the Whale: the Media from Parliament

Here's what it's like these days. I returned to our tiny Guardian office in Westminster to find three—count them, three—Liberal Democrat spin doctors clustered around.

They were like ants at a picnic. You'd leave one at the door, and find another waiting by your computer screen. As soon as you'd dealt with him, another would turn up over your shoulder.

'Did you like Paddy's intervention?' asked one. 'Wasn't he funny?'

'Jackie Ballard was terrific, wasn't she,' said another. 'She was so poised!'

'Look, here's a copy of what Blair actually said last year', said a third, and there was a photocopy of Hansard, proving beyond doubt that, as Leader of the Opposition, Mr Blair has described as mere 'sticking plaster', a sum of money larger than his own government proposes to spend on the NHS.

I suppose we ought to be flattered. Maybe we should be like those old theatre critics who used to drop phrases into their reviews hoping they'd appear on the posters ('I laughed till my prostate ached!'—Monty Maltravers, Daily Beast). This would provide publicity for them as well as for the show, implying that theirs' was the good opinion which everybody craved.

Ms Ballard could seek re-election in Taunton with similar quotes: 'Terrific . . . poised—the Guardian'; 'Ms Ballard is as welcome in Parliament as an Airwick in an abattoir—Daily Telegraph'.

Don't misunderstand me. All those three spin doctors are intelligent, thoughtful, well-informed young persons. It's a pleasure to do business with them. Their party should pay them huge sums of money.

But you have to wonder about the state of British politics, in which there is such an obsessional concern about these tiny soundbites from the smallest of the three main parties.

It's an aged cliché that nobody now has an attention span. But we do. The actual remark made in the House might last for only 10 seconds. But the debate over each single word is pursued for hours.

THIS is Simon Hoggart, of course (the *Guardian*, 6 November 1997). And this *is* what it's like these days. Walking along the media route between the Commons and Millbank one evening recently, I heard a couple of earnest young spinners discussing their day's work. 'I just wish', said one 'that we had gone the extra mile'. 'Yes', replied the other, 'I think we might have got GMTV'. But who is getting whom? And for what? More important still, what if anything can be done about it?

It is not possible to talk about any of this unless we have a reasonably clear idea what the political role of the media should be. The technology may be changing at a bewildering pace, but this makes it even more important to hang on to a firm sense of the civic role of the media in a democratic polity. If that sounds rather serious, then so it should. We need something against which to measure what is happening both to politicians and to the media, and consider what might be done about it. To suggest that something might need to be done is not to succumb to a form of golden-ageism. There is much to celebrate—the extension of choice, the explosion of information sources, the end of deference in broadcasting, the opinion pages of the broadsheets—but there is also much to be concerned about. This presents a challenge both for politicians and the media.

Back to the civic role. The media should be the place where a mass democracy communicates with itself. This involves a whole range of activities: informing, discussing, arguing, questioning, reflecting, investigating, exposing ... Without a media that performs this role, the nation is deprived of its collective street corner, market square and noticeboard. If deprived in this way, the quality of its democracy will suffer. This is recognised in what we traditionally say about the importance of a free press, the quasi-constitutional status that is bestowed upon the fourth estate, and the public service obligations imposed upon broadcasters. Either we still believe in what we say about all of this or we do not.

Of course there are difficulties, tensions, and contradictions. The public service requirements placed upon broadcasters (or some of them) are not matched by similar requirements (except weak and voluntary ones) placed upon the press. In the name of a free press, tabloid editors have been able to dispense with any notion of civic responsibility. Faced with the prospect of a balancing test between privacy and information of the kind contained in the provisions of the European Convention on Human Rights, most of the press have simply gone into denunciation mode. Yet a democratic society requires a press that is free *and* responsible. The fact that there are inevitable tensions here does not mean that a civic interest cannot be identified. The same applies to issues of ownership, quality and access across the media.

If we believe in the civic role of the media, there are disturbing developments around. Some come from politicians, others from the media themselves. Let's start with the politicians. They like to be thought well of and want to control the message and the messengers as far as possible. There is nothing new or even disreputable about this: it comes with the job. What is new, though, is the systematic and professional way in which it is now undertaken. The wearisome gibes about spinners and soundbites do capture the modern enterprise of news management that is central to contemporary politics. The practitioners of these black arts are increasingly the key figures in the political world. As communication flows are deliberately centralised, their authority as the source of information and opinion is further enhanced. Their task is to ensure that there is a coherent and consistent message and that everyone stays 'on message' in their dealings with the media. Labour honed these skills in opposition and has carried them into government. Political communication in Britain will never be the same again.

In party terms it represents a huge achievement. Anyone who remembers the shambles of the old Labour Party will scarcely complain about the fact that it has become the sleekest machine in town. Nor is this the only way in which today's politicians have seen the new opportunities for news management. Of course Peter Riddell is right to point to the various ways in which Parliament is losing its central place in political debate, but for politicians there have been compensating gains. The televising of Parliament has brought major new opportunities for self-presentation. Not only is this true for the party leaders in the gladiatorial encounters at Question Time, where phrases in search of headlines are routinely exchanged, but for the footsoldiers too. A single intervention in prime time is worth more than a string of worthy speeches in the long hours that follow.

Even just being there is enough, if carefully positioned. Politicians know that they can be beamed effortlessly into the living rooms of their constituents. A seat on the row just behind the front benches is the most prized spot, always remembering to nod vigorously in agreement with even the most banal statements. Then there is the clustering around questioners and speakers, with more nodding and general harrumphing, in full camera shot. The minority parties take this 'doughnuting' particularly seriously, often rushing members into the Chamber to fill a camera angle in order to give the appearance of massed strength, especially important when the clip is shown in Scotland, Wales or Northern Ireland. This is a reminder of the often neglected role of the local media. The fact that Scotland has its own national media system, whereas in Wales it is much weaker, was extremely important in the referendum campaigns.

When backbench politicians perform in Parliament, their real eye is frequently on their local media. This means both regional television and local newspapers. The regional television companies all have their Westminster presence and all have their space to fill, both in their news bulletins and their other slots (usually a weekly political programme in the case of the BBC regions). An intervention in the House of Commons is invariably a press release for the local media in the making ('MP challenges Minister on West Wittering hospital crisis'), while adjournment debates—not debates of course, just a lonely exchange between a Member and a Minister usually when everyone else has left—are a reliable way of raising local issues and attracting the attention of the local media. Press releases are far more effective than speeches in engaging local media interest and thereby conveying an impression of frenetic parliamentary activity on behalf of constituents. The growth of local free newspapers, paid for by advertising and delivered to every door, has been a major development as far as politicians are concerned. These free sheets routinely reproduce press releases verbatim, presenting an opportunity to politicians that they have not been slow to exploit.

So there is a paradox. The decline in the importance of Parliament, reflected in the waning media attention, has gone hand in hand with an expansion of the opportunities available to politicians to use their membership of the House of Commons for media purposes. A particularly nice example of this paradox is the way in which MPs are able to acquire video stills of themselves on their feet in the Commons Chamber for use in their campaign literature. In this sense, at least, the green benches still retain their importance. It plays to a mythology. So, in a different way, does the fact that some newspapers carry an annual report of the number of times that MPs have voted during a session. It is an absurd statistic, yet produces a culture among MPs in which they speak of 'keeping their voting record up' so that they will not fare badly in the newspaper league tables. Those Labour MPs currently enjoying their regular 'constituency weeks' may find that this is an unwelcome and unintended consequence of their authorised absence.

We may lament the way in which Parliament is treated by the media, but it is scarcely irrational or inexplicable. The decline in serious reporting of parliamentary debates, and its substitution with the lampooning of gallery sketchwriters, accurately reflects the changing character of Parliament itself. At a party to mark the first anniversary of the 1992 intake of Labour MPs, John Smith remarked that it was important to remember that the Commons was really an 'intimate theatre'. It is not surprising therefore that it attracts theatre reviewers rather than serious analysts. The only real remedy is for Parliament to make itself a more significant institution. There is a regular fuss from MPs about Ministers making statements in studios or press conferences rather than in Parliament, but this is a desperate clutching at past form rather than an engagement with present substance.

For argument, debate and investigation has gone elsewhere. For a Minister with something to hide, the Commons Chamber is much less intimidating than the Today Programme or Newsnight. Parliament becomes an echo chamber for issues and arguments generated in the media. The Nolan Committee was invented because the Commons could not deal with matters of parliamentary conduct that the media had exposed; and the Scott inquiry was initiated after the Commons had failed to make progress with an inquiry of its own. Ministers now resign, not because of the traditional canons of ministerial responsibility to Parliament, but because the media have success-fully claimed their scalp. It is difficult to blame the media for neglecting or trivialising Parliament, when Parliament has allowed itself to become neglected and trivialised. Even the 'great parliamentary moments' are not what they once were, largely confined to dramatic resignation statements (Norman Lamont, Geoffrey Howe) that are conventionally delivered to the Commons first.

Who wants to change?

The media will only have to start taking Parliament seriously when Parliament starts taking itself seriously. It is not difficult to come up with a list of reforms that would help to bring this about—they all involve making it less easy for the Commons to be rolled over routinely by the executive steam-roller—but it is difficult to see how these are to be achieved without wider political reforms. What is being suggested here though, and what is much less noticed, is the way in which politicians are complicit in what is happening—despite protestations about their desire for reform—because of the way in which the present arrangements enable them to make use of the media for their own political purposes. They are now equipped with daily press releases on which they are required only to fill in their name. They are supplied with more money to run their offices, which they can use to run a permanent election campaign in their local media or buy the computers on which they can target subsets of voters. It may not be very edifying, nor have much to do with the glories of parliamentary democracy, but it does help to explain why there are compensations for politicians in the way they are treated by the media. It may also help to explain why the 'incumbency' advantage of sitting politicians seems to be increasing; and why the decline in public regard for politicians in general looks rather different when people are asked about their own Members of Parliament.

So much for the politicians. They have increasingly become professional media managers, in different ways and at different levels, and it is entirely sensible from their point of view that this should be the case. The problem arises only in relation to the effects on the civic role of the media. It can compress and stifle debate, reducing political communication to the crudest kind of propaganda. The ability of the media to counteract this tendency is reduced by the extent to which journalists also become complicit in the process. As political communication flows are centralised, with a small number of key gatekeepers, not only is access to other sources restricted, but a relationship of dependency can develop. When set alongside some of the other trends in the media of the kind described by Peter Riddell, there is certainly cause for concern.

This goes beyond the sheer awfulness of the tabloids at their worst. Their abandonment of public issues in favour of private titillations has a corrosive effect on civic life. What the *Sun* would have done with Gladstone's nocturnal activities (and erotic diaries) is too appalling to contemplate. We are fast reaching a point when nobody who cares about preserving a private life will want to go anywhere near politics. This may turn out to be the durable contribution of the tabloids to our democracy; either this or a political reaction of a kind that damages the legitimate freedoms of the press. It is not just what is being done, but the loss of what might be done instead. If the tabloids set about popularising the real public issues, or devoting their investigative resources to all those matters that need investigating, then their civic role would be transformed. Some chance. It is far more likely that politicians will want to appease the tabloid agenda.

It may be that debasement, trivialisation and irresponsibility is the price that we have to pay for a free press. In an important sense this must be so. Yet this does not mean that it is either impossible or undesirable to put a public interest framework of some kind around the press, above all in relation to the balance between privacy and intrusion. Either this will happen through effective self-regulation by the Press Complaints Commission, or through judges using the balancing provisions of the European Convention on Human Rights, or through a new privacy law passed by Parliament. There is room for argument about the respective merits and demerits of these different approaches. Where there is no room for argument is on the need for a satisfactory public interest framework. The same applies to the need to ensure that the diversity of the press, fundamental to a democracy, is sustained against monopolistic tendencies. If market power is used unfairly to drive out competitors and diminish diversity (the charge made against the predatory pricing tactics of the Murdoch empire), then there is a clear public interest in making sure that this does not happen.

More technologies, less argument?

Similar considerations apply to the new broadcasting technologies, where it is the task of the state to ensure that the terms of access are not controlled by those who own the technology. But some of the current trends in broadcasting raise other issues too. It is not necessary to believe that a general dumbing down is in full swing to think that the democratic role of the media is weakened by some of the prevailing tendencies in broadcasting. The fear of joined-up argument among broadcasters marches hand in hand with the soundbite syndrome among politicians. The effect is to create an episodic jumble of talking heads. The sterile adversarialism of British politics is too often simply reinforced by the broadcast media. Where is the space within which ideas can be discussed and arguments developed? It is no doubt easier to treat the issue of European monetary union in terms of party splits rather than as a challenge in explanation (just to take a leading example), but it represents a bias against understanding with a vengeance.

If politicians have to do politics differently, then so too do the broadcasters. Indeed, the broadcasters have a crucial role to play in bringing this about. If their escape from an old deference was a precondition for this, the conversion of politics into light entertainment represents an opposite danger. At present it remains only a danger, but a real one. When some of the current trends are logged—the decline of documentaries on the ITV network, the recurrent desire to shift *News at Ten* to a less pivotal place in the schedules, the BBC plan to disengage from some of its parliamentary programmes—it is difficult not to feel that a retreat is in progress. Developments of this kind are far more serious for the quality of our democracy than the complaints by politicians that some broadcasters now just want to beat them up on air. It is the job of the broadcasters to give politicians a hard time; but it is also the job of public service broadcasting to ensure that arguments and voices are heard. There are inevitable and wholly welcome tensions here.

But who speaks for the public interest in all of this? In crucial areas nobody does. There is a deficiency here that requires attention and remedy. This is well illustrated by the example of election broadcasting. We know that broadcasting, above all television, provides the main route through which voters learn about election issues and shape their electoral judgments. This is not because voters like watching election television, but because they like watching television and therefore get elections. So it matters hugely, which is why it receives such obsessive political attention. Yet the arrangements under which election broadcasting take place are a curious mix of formal rules and informal agreements between parties and broadcasters. It is difficult to claim that what results is what the public needs. There are much better models available (of the kind to be found long ago in Jay Blumler's little book on *The Challenge of Election Broadcasting*), in which the right of politicians to make their case is linked to a duty to have that case critically examined. The parties may not like this, but the public interest would be better served by it.

Similar considerations apply to the ritual exchanges on the eve of general elections between the party leaders, and between the parties and the broadcasters, on the question of whether there should be televised debates between the leaders. We have to endure the wearisome on-off stories about who is running scared of whom. Yet there is surely a clear public interest in matching Prime Ministers, current and putative, against each other in televised debate under rules designed to allow arguments to be tested and judgments made. There is currently no mechanism through which this public interest can be asserted. Our uncodified make-it-up-as-we-go-along kind of constitutional arrangements are here reflected in the lack of rules and machinery for the conduct of election broadcasting.

The remedy is an independent commission with responsibility for all aspects of electoral conduct, including broadcasting. This should be seen as an integral part of the political reform programme that the Blair Government is implementing, sitting alongside those other areas (such as party funding) where independent rules are slowly replacing informal practices. A commission of this kind could take the whole of party political broadcasting under its wing, as this is really part of a permanent election campaign and there are soon to be many more elections and referendums. The broadcasters have recently proposed an end to party political broadcasts outside elections. The politicians (or at least some of them) have responded by asserting their right to communicate directly with the electorate. There are good rival claims involved here. The broadcasters are right to want to banish items of crude propaganda that viewers dislike. The politicians are right to assert the importance of unmediated political communication. But where both are wrong is in thinking that such matters should be settled either by unilateral declaration or by brokered deal. It is possible to find a model that meets the different objectives, but this requires a public interest framework of a kind that an independent commission would provide.

The larger and longer question, extending far beyond specific issues such as election broadcasting, is whether a public interest framework of any kind will be achievable in the new media age that lies immediately ahead. In particular, can the civic role of the media be sustained and developed, or is it doomed to wither and die? The answer is entirely unclear. It is possible to be either chirpily optimistic or gloomily pessimistic about the prospects. One kind of future looks replete with democratic opportunities; another kind represents a form of civic death. What is at stake is the ability of the media to continue to perform the functions in a democratic society that have traditionally been assigned to them. It is clear that a period of media history is coming to an end. Whatever the particular criticisms that can be made of it, in Britain it has been a period in which the media—above all, in the form of public service broadcasting—have played a notable civic role and made a significant democratic contribution. What is not clear is how, or even whether, this will be possible in the future.

On the pessimistic view, the deterioration that is already apparent is set to intensify dramatically. The fragmented multichannel future represents the end of a common arena in which issues of shared concern are discussed and public figures interrogated. A general conversation is replaced by disconnected babble. The continuing dialogue that is essential to democratic politics is crowded out by the media ghettos of particular interests. Broadcasting becomes a choice between undifferentiated pap or narrow sectionalism, while newspapers continue to shift remorselessly away from hard news and analysis to softer 'lifestyle' and gossip. The implications for political life of such developments are very serious. An environment is created in which the media enable citizens to escape from the domain of public life altogether, while politicians further hone their skills of media manipulation to send messages of slick simplicity at moments of political choice. In such a future the idea of an informed democracy becomes a bad joke.

More technologies, more democracy?

The optimistic prospect looks radically different from this. Digital broadcasting brings with it a huge expansion of choice and diversity. Alongside government on-line, electronic democracy and the rich resources of the internet, the new media age opens up exciting civic possibilities. A pluralist democracy is sustained by a vigorously plural media system. In place of an era in which political broadcasting has been strictly rationed and controlled, there arrives a period in which the whole range of positions can be represented and all views expressed. Dedicated channels, partisan and specialist, enable both majorities and minorities to be heard. Arguments and opinions can be explored fully. Local radio and television will provide major new opportunities for local issues to be discussed. In all these ways the prospect is of a political culture that is energised and a democracy that is enriched. As the political system itself is changed, with power decentralised and new sites for democracy opened up, a media system that matches this change becomes a crucial source of new civic energy.

These are compelling alternative futures. It is useful to set them out, if only to bring into sharp relief what is at stake. Of course matters are unlikely to be as clear-cut as this in practice. Elements of each will no doubt come together to shape a new mixed economy in the media. But it should not be a question merely of waiting to see what happens. Public policy in a democracy has a responsibility to ensure that the framework exists in which the civic role of the media can be sustained and developed. At a time when there are both threats and opportunities on a dramatic scale, it has never been more important to get this framework right.

Biographical Note

The author is Labour MP for Cannock Chase, and joint editor of *The Political Quarterly*.

Themes and Threnodies in Contemporary Satire

MARTIN ROWSON

In the years up to the 1997 general election, many people imagined Britain to be going through a golden age of satire. As the Major Government sank deeper and deeper into scandal and crisis, it frequently seemed as if it were trying to outstrip satire itself, punchdrunkenly wrapping itself in inverted commas to become Britain's first ironic, post-modern government. Indeed, with the BSE crisis—where, as a result of obsessional and dogmatic de-regulation, our national dish had been rendered not only poisonous but also likely to drive you mad and then kill you—the government was in real danger of entering the realm of meta-satire. You couldn't, as they say, make it up. More to the point, Swift and Hogarth couldn't have made it up. All that was meant to change after 1st May 1997. The death of Diana, Princess of Wales in August of the same year was seen as reinforcing the point. The Age of Cynicism was over, even as we cried in the streets, we came to feel more at ease with ourselves. Satire was, not for the first time, dead. Some hope.

Biographical Note

Martin Rowson is one of Britain's leading political cartoonists. His work appears regularly in the *Guardian, Mirror, Independent on Sunday, The Observer, Express, Time Out* and *Tribune*. He has also produced comic book versions of T. S. Eliot's 'The Waste Land' and Lawrence Sterne's 'Tristram Shandy', as well as illustrating books by Will Self and John Sweeney. In June 1998 he held a one-man exhibition of cartoons on New Labour opened by Peter Mandelson.

© The Political Quarterly Publishing Co. Ltd. 1998
Published by Blackwell Publishers, 108 Cowley Road, Oxford OX4 1JF, UK and 350 Main Street, Malden, MA 02148, USA

Broadcasting Policy and the Digital Revolution

ANDREW GRAHAM

BROADCASTING policy is currently dominated by three propositions on which there is a dangerous near unanimity. First, broadcasting (along with printing, publishing and telecommunications) is undergoing a technological revolution. Second, since it is impossible to predict exactly what form this revolution will take, 'the market should be left to develop unhindered' (as the consultant's KPMG argued in their report to the European Commission). Third, this revolution will inevitably bring more radio and television channels and this, in its turn, will necessarily mean that the old world of state monopolised broadcasting will be replaced by a new and better world of free competition and extended choice.

The appeal of these propositions is obvious. If what is inevitable is also desirable, how fortunate. No further thought is required.

Here I take a directly contrary position. While welcoming the technical change, I shall demonstrate that propositions two and three are based neither on logic, nor on empirical research, nor on economic analysis. Rather they are the result of mistaken understandings about (a) how the new technology affects the economics of broadcasting, (b) how the theory of economic choice and competition really work, and (c) the very particular role played by the media in a democratic society. Having cleared the errors out of the way, I then suggest the main directions in which broadcasting policy *ought* to be moving.

The New Technology—from Analogue to Digital

One major reason why the arguments above are so widely believed is that many people are swept along by the new technology without really understanding what is taking place. However, if we strip away the mystique, the underlying technological forces are quite simple. Two things are happening at the same time, each making the other possible in a reinforcing process. One is the move from machines that were analogue to machines that are digital. The other is the exponential increase in power of the digital machines.

Let us unpack this a stage further and see what it means for broadcasting. The world that we experience directly is a place of gradual change, not one of sudden jumps. Speed, temperature, heat, colour and sound all change continuously, not discretely. As a result it was natural that, at first, scientists should have modelled the world in a similar (or analogous) manner. Early machines therefore consisted of wheels, pumps, levers and needles, all of

© The Political Quarterly Publishing Co. Ltd. 1998
Published by Blackwell Publishers, 108 Cowley Road, Oxford OX4 1JF, UK and 350 Main Street, Malden, MA 02148, USA

which move *gradually*. Analogue forms of measurement also happen to be very efficient at conveying information to human beings—a speedometer in the form of a dial is much easier to read than a set of numbers.

Analogue information is easy to read, but not to transmit or reproduce with great accuracy: '50 out of 100' is far more exact than the fact that a needle on a dial is 'about half way round'. One of the key aspects of the digital revolution has, therefore, been the desire to measure everything *precisely*—a desire now realisable as a result of the persistent and extraordinary increase in the power of digital computers.

Once digital computers are able to process large numbers quickly, then measurements can be recorded so minutely that change *appears gradual*; at which point the digital computer can do everything that was previously done in an analogue form only far more accurately. Your speedometer may look as if it is 'about half way round', but, underneath, the speed is being recorded as 50.235 mph (or whatever level of accuracy you require).

The ability to *measure everything* digitally is the digital revolution. If everything can be represented by a number, then as far as the computer is concerned, sound, heat, colour and temperature are, technically, all the same. Moreover, if sound and light can be represented by numbers so also can pictures, music and text. Moving the 0s and 1s that stand for musical notes is identical to moving those that stand for letters of the alphabet, so text and music can be intermingled. Music or pictures can also be processed (edited, combined with other material, copied, and erased) in just the same way as words. This is multimedia. And, provided that standards can be agreed so that the digital signals can be moved from machine to machine, the ability to combine all these is the major force creating convergence.

Digital broadcasting is about to bring all of this to radio and television and, when it does, the ability to squeeze more and more information into less and less will allow an explosion of channels. Of greater longer term importance is the fact that once television signals, and then eventually the TV set, go digital there will be vastly greater scope for interactivity. The effects are potentially largest where the signals come via cable, because fibre optic cables can carry several hundred channels at once and do so fully interactively, but similar effects will occur with digital terrestrial broadcasting and digital satellite broadcasting. They will also be able to handle far more channels than in the past, and many of them will have some capacity for interaction by linking to the telephone as the return path.

Thus far, the widely held views that the new technology is powerful, all pervasive, causing strong forces towards convergence and creating the possibility for many more channels is totally justified. Also justified is the view that technology has been (and will be) the major factor making everything, well almost everything, cheaper.

The Flaws in the Argument

Where then do the arguments start to go wrong? The errors arise initially from not following through the implications of the digital revolution for the economics of broadcasting.

The first implication of the digital revolution is that the economies of scale of broadcasting will be intensified. It is already true under analogue broadcasting that distributing a programme to more people costs very little *extra*, but with digital broadcasting a perfect copy of any programme can be sent anywhere in the world for near zero cost. In other words, the gap between 'first copy' and 'second copy' costs will increase—hence there are massive economies of scale.

A further reason why this gap will rise is that, despite the massive technological improvements, the *fixed* costs of making programmes are not falling as fast as might be supposed. Indeed in some cases they are rising. This is because of two factors. One is that the major component of fixed costs is not equipment, but people, and not just individual people, but *teams* of people. Thus, especially in the complex world of global multimedia, programmes of any quality will have high fixed costs. The other is that the global competition brought about by the new technology is pushing up the price of scarce talent. The stars of stage and screen have always been able to earn a rent for their scarcity, but globalisation is dramatically increasing such rent. As a result the old monopoly of spectrum scarcity is being replaced by a new monopoly of available talent. The results can already be seen in the escalating fees paid for sports rights.

The second implication of the digital revolution is that there will be an increase in 'economies of scope'. These arise when activities in one area either decrease costs or increase revenues in a second area. This, of course, is precisely what the convergence of printing, publishing, telecommunications, computing and broadcasting is all about. Stories collected for a newspaper can be repackaged at very low cost for broadcasting and material collected for a broadcast can be reissued as a CD or incorporated into multimedia publishing.

The third implication is that there will be a vast increase in the benefits of being in a network. This is because in order for the full benefits of convergence to be achieved, information must be moved around in accordance with a set of standards—the standards of that network—so that everything is interoperable. But no-one will want to join a network or a standard that looks a loser (as Betamax found with VHS and as Apple is finding now with Microsoft). The firm that will win in a network battle is therefore the one that manages to acquire the critical mass. In the economics of networks there are no second prizes. The winner takes all.

There is a fourth implication which follows from the first three: the media will become far *more* concentrated, *not* less so. In order to benefit from economies of scale it will be essential to be large as possible, to benefit from economies of scope to have fingers in as many pies as possible and for networks to work well someone—and it will mostly be just *one* firm—has to set and control the standards.

This is not just theory. It is already happening. In the last few years Disney, Time Warner, Viacom, Paramount, Turner Broadcasting and Bertelsmann, to name but a few, have all been engaged in enormous multimedia mergers or acquisitions. Murdoch has spread his interests both globally and industrially and, in computers, Microsoft's operating systems have set the standards and dominated the industry. Even the Internet, long held up as the symbol of easy entry and competition, is joining the world of big players. America Online (AOL) took a decade to reach one million customers, but in just the last two years has jumped to ten million.

These implications are a far cry from the view that the future of broadcasting will be one in which state monopolies give way to a world of free competition. There will undoubtedly be more channels, but there will also be *fewer* owners. State monopolies may be undesirable but exchanging them for private monopolies is hardly desirable in *any* industry. However, there are more serious issues still to come. To see why we have to consider another feature of the new technology: the role of electronic programme guides and their importance as controller of the gateway.

Electronic Programme Guides and the Control of Gateways

Once television is broadcast in a digital form, the same amount of spectrum will be able to contain several 'channels'. Each multiplex (as the new form of broadcasters are called) will therefore contain the capacity to transmit *multiple* programmes simultaneously in a single stream of digital bits. In order for a *particular* programme to be seen by the viewer the TV has to be set to select a programme, *not* a channel.

What this means is that one or more 'Electronic Programme Guides' (or EPGs) will be broadcast all the time. Moreover, it is the EPG which will be the first thing any particular set will automatically select when first switched on. Viewers will then use a handset to pick one of the programmes on offer. Instead of pressing buttons to obtain a channel, it will be more like using a mouse on a computer to select a file.

There are two fundamentally different ways in which these EPGs will be important. One concerns the technology, the other the economics of choice and competition.

At the *technical* level the EPG will be part and parcel of what is called the Conditional Access System (or CAS). This is the software and hardware that will be in the set-top box (or soon built into the TV). This box will carry out a variety of functions, but the important point is that for the first time televisions will have the equivalent of an operating system. They will not be as complex as those of computers, at least not at first, but potentially they are every bit as important in the battle for control.

Few consumers will buy more than one set-top box. Just adding a second smart card to a single CAS will probably nearly double the installed cost (from £150 to £250) and adding a second CAS will probably nearly double the cost again.[1] Moreover, quite apart from the cost, consumers have, quite rightly, shown themselves extremely resistant to multiple incompatible systems. Similarly no broadcaster will broadcast more than one EPG. This is because even a relatively simple EPG is the equivalent of broadcasting another full channel, so the loss of revenue is high. In addition, for all the reasons given earlier about the economics of networks, one set-top box is likely to dominate the market. There may be an initial period with several, but eventually a single standard will predominate.

It follows that, if any one consumer buys only one CAS and if each supplier of a CAS would choose to show only one EPG, then any one consumer will be dependent on a single EPG and, via this, on whoever controls that EPG. Moreover, the fixed costs that the consumer incurs (plus, in the case of aerials, the physically fixed parts) make switching an unrealistic possibility over a wide range of prices. Both economics and natural consumer inertia therefore mean that each consumer, once they have made their initial purchase, will thereafter face a *de facto* monopoly of 100 per cent. It will be as if, having bought a Tesco store card, it would be impossible to shop anywhere else— except by paying a fine of several hundreds of pounds.

The monopoly control of this crucial gateway must be a matter of concern just because it is a monopoly. This is hardly a case in which 'the market should be left to develop unhindered'.

Fortunately, at least in the UK, this point has been addressed by the Independent Television Commission who have published a code of conduct for EPGs which all broadcasters will be required to follow. The primary purposes of this code are to ensure (a) that any broadcaster will be able to have their programmes shown via any set-top box and (b) that the design of the EPGs should not hinder competition. This is welcome, but it is far from enough.

To see why the regulation of the ITC is insufficient it is necessary to turn to the *content* of the EPGs and to re-examine the assumptions upon which the theory of economic choice and competition relies. Two of these assumptions are core. The first is that competition only works properly when there are a large number of firms, none of them large enough to dominate the market. This has been shown above to be most unlikely.

The second assumption, even more fundamental to the theory of consumer choice, is that consumers *know and understand* both the *full list* of items that are on sale and *all the prices* of these items. If consumers do not have this information they cannot choose rationally and firms, even where there are large numbers of them, are not really in competition with one another. They can just trade on 'islands of ignorance'. Of course we know that when people are born they do not have this information. Nevertheless they learn quite rapidly. In particular they learn language and, as Bacharach has shown[2], sharing a common view of the meaning of words is a central requirement for the buying and selling of goods in the modern world. For example, when we order a pizza by 'phone, it is not *that* pizza *right there* that is ordered, but what each of us understands implicitly by the word 'pizza'. After a period of time in a relatively stable world such knowledge may be widespread and become 'common knowledge' (what everyone knows that everyone knows).

This is fine as far as the selling of many goods and services is concerned, though less so when technology and society are changing rapidly. However, it will always be a difficult assumption to apply to broadcasting, since the one thing you cannot do with a broadcast is pick it up and inspect it before consuming it. But these points pale into insignificance as compared with the problems that arise with EPGs. It is manifestly absurd to assume perfect information in the context of EPGs, since these will not only be a new way of giving people information, but will also be giving people information about information! As a result to put the enhancement of competition before the provision of information, as the legislation implicitly does at present, is to put the cart before the horse.

Externalities, Merit Goods, Community and Democracy[3]

There are four further flaws in the argument that market driven choice will give us the broadcasting that we all need and want. These flaws all occur because the market does not always reflect what society needs and they all apply even where *the market is well informed and competitive*. They are therefore *additional* to the problems of concentration and to the special problems of EPGs already mentioned.

The first flaw arises where there are 'externalities'. These occur whenever there are costs or benefits that are not captured via the market (e.g. exhaust fumes that choke pedestrians). In the case of broadcasting, an analogous argument can be made about the portrayal of excessive violence having a negative externality if it makes people feel more fearful. Alternatively many of the externalities of broadcasting are beneficial. For example, positive externalities will occur if programmes promote 'common knowledge'. Shared language is the most obvious example, but such externalities also include all kinds of scientific or even social knowledge, such as the right number to dial in an emergency. Positive externalities may also arise where broadcasting contributes towards a greater understanding of, and tolerance towards, different groups in society. The important point, however, is not which externalities are positive or negative, but that neither are taken into account by the market.

The second flaw occurs because some of broadcasting is a 'merit good'. These are goods, such as preventative health care, from which we benefit in the long run, but which, left to our own devices, we are unlikely to take fully into account in our immediate decisions. As a result neither health care nor education are left entirely to the market. Broadcasting has a similar capacity to extend our knowledge, our capacities and our imaginations—and in ways that we may not immediately realise.

The third problem with the market as a method of allocating goods and services is that it merely aggregates *individual* preferences. As a result, *by definition*, it does not take account of the value of events that have intrinsic value from being shared, from people being part of a community and from doing things *together*. For example, for many people the fact that *others* are standing silent at eleven o'clock on Remembrance Sunday is part of what makes them feel part of a society. And many would regard it as morally repugnant if, in order to pay one's respects, one had to *pay*.

The fourth flaw with the market is that it is a basic principle of a democratic society that votes should not be bought and sold. This alone is sufficient justification for broadcasting not to be provided entirely commercially. Moreover, for a democracy to function properly it is not just a question of votes every five years or so, but the deeper question of how individuals in society become autonomous human beings. As Isaiah Berlin noted, people have not only the negative right to liberty (the freedom 'from') but a set of positive rights (the freedom 'to') without which they cannot participate fully in society and without which any claim by a society that it is democratic is a sham. Such rights are not the domain of the market.

The final point to be noted about this set of flaws is that, far from the new technology diminishing their importance, it increases it. As convergence occurs and as the Information Society develops increasing amounts of interactivity, functions as diverse as shopping, banking, visiting an estate agent, consulting a doctor, booking a holiday, taking out a pension, obtaining a degree or contacting the emergency services may all start (and in some cases end) with the TV (or whatever the TV and the computer will within a few years have become). Of course there will be other sources of contact and information about all of these, but the convenience of television, its ubiquity and, in the near future, the ability to interact with it, will mean that for many people the TV will often be their first point of contact—effectively the EPGs will be their Reception Service on the Information Superhighway.

Moreover EPGs could be much more influential than a reception service. They will set the agenda and, by highlighting some things rather than others, they will have the ability to guide both consumers and citizens to the areas the designer of the EPG wishes them to see first. Indeed as EPGs become more sophisticated they will become a major marketing and advertising tool. Search engines on the World Wide Web have already become a major site for advertising—and, while it is difficult to identify the precise effects of marketing and advertising, no one has ever maintained that all of this effort and expenditure was of no avail. So important are these EPGs likely to be, that, in the UK, the digital satellite system BSkyB is planning is expected to devote more than 30Mbps to its EPG. This is the equivalent of more than five full channels. It is hard to imagine that such a massive commitment of resources is being done with no thought except the promotion of the public interest. What is needed from a public interest point of view is a source of information that is impartial and trusted. Not what we are likely to get if it is left to the proprietary interests of the market.

The Central Dilemmas for Public Policy

Public policy for broadcasting faces a number of dilemmas. Two of these are familiar in industrial economics. One is the conflict between, on the one hand, the desire for low costs per unit (production efficiency) that go with economies of scale and dominance and, on the other hand, the desire to keep prices close to costs by competition (consumption efficiency). The other is the conflict between efficiency now and efficiency over time. For consumption efficiency now we want intense competition, but the industry may prosper better if a degree of monopoly is allowed while the industry gets established.

The third dilemma is political. Consumers like freedom of choice and the increase in channels that the new technology will make possible. However, the analysis above has shown that the same technology that brings us many channels also creates forces that lead to concentration of ownership. The plurality of editorial control that is so essential to democracy is not therefore likely to follow from totally free choice. If we care about our democracy some other solution has to be found.

Closely related to this is a fourth dilemma: the conflicting requirements of choice, quality and access. An increase in channels implies fragmentation of audiences. But lower audiences imply either lower revenue or higher prices. This is in direct conflict with the desire for high quality programmes accessible to all. High quality programmes require high fixed costs, but the cost *per viewer* can still be very low provided that there are large audiences. The trouble is that, within the market, there is no incentive to recognise this. Everyone thinks they can 'free ride', migrating away to their special interest programmes without this having any effect on the core programmes. It is just as if, in a club, members want to buy each of the facilities, but are not willing to contribute to the cost of the building. Of course in a full free market some high quality programmes would be made, but many of these would only be available at high prices. What is more in a commercial world that is looking for short-term returns, even these would be likely to be dominated by the incumbency of existing tastes.

The final dilemma is that between the desire to promote competition and the desire to provide information. As we have seen, competition only works properly when consumers are well informed. Yet, under the new technology, the provision of that information comes via the EPGs where there is a danger of proprietary control.

Andrew Graham

Broadcasting Policy in the Digital Age

The starting point in framing contemporary broadcasting policy has to be the new technology and the opportunities that this is creating for far more diverse forms of television. Already many households have two or more sets and once these sets go both digital and interactive uses will arise which at the moment are hardly imaginable. These new opportunities are welcome. They also change what is desirable for regulation. Some of what is received will be an extension of today's Internet and, just as the content of today's private 'snail mail' is left almost entirely unregulated, so too should some parts of tomorrow's television. Unregulated that is by any public body: parents might well want to operate a decentralised and personalised form of regulation over what their children can and cannot access (something which the technology can make possible relatively easily).

The new technology also alters the context within which any regulation has to operate. In the past much of the effectiveness of British broadcasting policy depended upon three factors which have either gone or are going. First, many of the key people had shared assumptions, since many of those in the commercial sector had been trained by and/or spent part of their careers with the BBC. Second, the so-called 'cosy duopoly' of the BBC and the ITV companies in which each sector had plenty of revenue without having to try too hard allowed 'light touch' regulation to be relatively successful. Successful, in particular, at producing high quality television, though much less successful in containing its costs. In contrast, when the pressure to compete is more intense, as it is now with more channels, with satellite and cable and with the commercial companies traded on the stock market, so also is there greater pressure to find ways round the regulation or to avoid some of the less well defined 'public service obligations'. Third, although this can be exaggerated, the media is increasingly open to global competition.

None of the above considerations, however, means that we should resort to a wholly free market across the whole of broadcasting. Indeed, many reasons have been given above why this would be a gross mistake. Faced with this situation the Peacock Committee, and in particular Sam Brittan, have suggested that there should be a Public Service Broadcasting Council (a PBC) which would purchase just those programmes which society collectively wants, but which the market itself would not elicit. The remainder of television would be sold either on a subscription basis or pay-per-view. They favoured this solution partly on the grounds that the majority of television would then be responding more directly to consumer demand, partly because this would make the public intervention specific, and partly because of what they saw as the implicit censorship of the BBC.

The problem with this view is that it fails to take into account the extent and nature of the market failures that need to be tackled. High quality programmes are not genre specific nor are externalities nor the sense of a set of interlinked communities. Having respect for other cultures so that they are displayed authentically rather than stereotypically ought to be something that we should expect in comedy and in soap dramas just as much as in news or documentaries. Of course these 'public interest' considerations are obligations that we might wish to see imposed on *all* channels, but these are just the 'fuzzy' edged kinds of regulations that will be the most difficult to sustain in the new competitive environment. All the more important, therefore, to sustain them *somewhere*.

Furthermore, a series of independent producers relying for their existence on the whims of a PBC is quite beside the point. There is no hope that such an arrangement could sustain the set of values, the non-market values, that need to exist alongside the market if we are to receive the broadcasting we want. As Denis Potter commented in his final interview with Melvyn Bragg, without the BBC no one else would have supported him long enough for him to have become the successful writer for television that he was.

This line of thinking is reinforced by the findings of the Bertelsmann Foundation. Following a wide-ranging investigation of broadcasting in ten countries in 1994 and 1995 they concluded that 'responsibility in programming has a chance only if and when it has been defined and constantly pursued as a strategic aim in the management [of the broadcaster]'.[4] It is difficult to see how both profitability and responsibility can be *constant* strategic aims *at the same time*. In the competitive market place profitability is bound to take priority, especially in the more aggressive environment that the new technology is now creating.

The implication of these arguments is that at least one important part of broadcasting policy should be the continuation of public service broadcasting. But this is not the public service broadcasting of the past. Notwithstanding its general high quality, this was a far too protected environment. Moreover, the Peacock Committee were right in their view that the old world of spectrum scarcity gave the BBC and the IBA the power to censor, a power that at times made 'high quality' look as if it was indeed being handed down from 'on high' to a public that was expected to be both docile and grateful: 'artificial pearls before real swine' as it has been offensively described.

Both the form of, and the case for, public service broadcasting being advocated here is quite different. In the world of channel plenty and the multicasting of the Internet of the next millennium, no one will be prevented from making and sending out any programme they want (provided it is not illegal). What is more and what is fundamental is that the *purposes* which public service broadcasting would be fulfilling are *additional to the market*. They would therefore widen choice, not narrow it. An institution whose purpose is to help ensure that all citizens enjoy Berlin's positive rights is the very opposite of censorship.

Two further arguments reinforce the conclusion that trying to structure the market via a significant amount of public service broadcasting is the right way forward. One is that we are *not* dealing just with an *industrial* problem. If we were, then the conflicts between production efficiency and consumption efficiency and between efficiency today versus efficiency tomorrow would be best handled with normal regulation, as has been done, for example, with Oftel, Ofgas and Ofwat. That is not the case here. The main problem with concentration in broadcasting is not the monopoly prices that would be charged, important though this is, but the threat to political diversity. This is hardly something that one can leave until later as some have argued. Moreover, 'political diversity' here means not just a diversity about party politics, but a deeper and broader spread of opinion about life, culture and society. The difficulty is that it is extremely difficult to legislate in favour of diversity. A regulator can hold down prices. They can even require impartiality; but for diversity to arise there has to be a *source* (or sources) for that diversity. In short there have to be one or more institutions who have that as one of their purposes.

The other advantage of the existence of one or more public service broadcasters is that this would tackle head on the dilemma between quality, fragmentation and access. As noted earlier, quality programmes have high fixed costs and these have to be covered somehow. Seen from this perspective the licence fee should not be regarded as 'the financing of public service broadcasting', but as the financing of *high quality with access for all*. Whether the BBC is currently doing this is both debatable and beyond the coverage of this paper, but the important point is the design of the system. The attraction of the licence fee is not only that it covers the fixed costs, but also that it solves the problem of free riding. Moreover, everyone then gets the opportunity to watch high quality programmes (including some that are 'merit goods') free at the point of consumption, as they should when marginal costs are near zero and when the goods are 'merit' goods.

Of course, the existence of public service broadcasters does not imply that all other forms of regulation should be dispensed with. Regulation designed to protect standards of taste and decency still have a role to play, though not necessarily on all channels nor at all on some of the forms of multicasting that will be possible. Such regulation is entirely complementary to public broadcasting. Moreover, at the time at which franchises are being allocated, there may still be a role for bodies such as the ITC to take account of some of the positive requirements mentioned above, though, for the reasons given earlier, such regulatory obligations are likely to be less effective than in the past.

Beyond this are two other ways in which broadcasting policy needs modernising. One must be to address properly the public interest aspects of EPGs. As explained, EPGs are likely to become the reception service as you enter the Information Society's one-stop-shop, entertainment, advice, counselling and education centre. The key requirement of an EPG must therefore be that the maximum number of people are as fully informed as possible. This puts a premium on making the system as simple as possible and, above all, as 'familiar' as possible. An EPG designed on this basis would look quite different from one designed to be competitively neutral, let alone one left to the wishes of a single proprietary supplier.

The final area in which broadcasting policy needs modernising is in its approach to **interactivity.** So far the arguments have been almost entirely confined to broadcasters acting in an entirely traditional way as a *national* delivery system of *one way* services. However, much remains to be done as broadcasting goes interactive. Here I touch on just two aspects. One deals with people's concern to have control over their own lives, the other with trusted sources of information: issues that are not unrelated.

There has been much discussion of the globalisation of the media. This is undoubtedly occurring. However, there are simultaneous pressures in the opposite direction. At the same time as the European Union is being reinforced, we are decentralising power to Scotland and Wales. The new technology, if deployed and used intelligently, has the capacity to respond to both of these trends. For example, with interactivity, with a multiplicity of channels and with the costs for making some (but not all) programmes falling rapidly, there is much more scope for local channels to discuss the issues that directly relate to people's lives. Planning inquiries or the potential closure of a school or the facilities offered by a hospital could all be the subject of interactive local broadcasting. In effect the new technology has the capacity to generate new forms of public space. Both commercial and public service broadcasters should contribute to such space. What is more this local content would go some way to offset the feeling, which many people have, that the new media is promoting a single global culture.

However, if this interactive space is to work effectively, some of it will need 'moderators' or 'editors' of discussion. To some people to speak of such functions may seem either unnecessary (on the grounds that the new technology provides access direct to information without the need for intermediaries) or undesirable (on the grounds that it smacks, again, of censorship). Such views are understandable, but they are deeply mistaken. The problem is that there is no such thing as pure or direct information. Information always has to be sifted and added to other information and to be put into some sort of order before it makes sense. Direct information is just noise, not knowledge.

Making sense of information is some people's job, but it is not and it never will be everyone's job. To suppose otherwise is to deny the division of labour. Once this point is accepted what matters is that some (though certainly not all) of the moderators and editors should be people whose main responsibility would be to promote common knowledge and public understanding. What the new media therefore needs, if it is to be widely accepted as a source of information and as a place for democratic discussion, is a set of *trusted third parties*, though I clearly use this term in a different sense from that used in electronic commerce.

Finally, lest there be any doubt, none of the policies advocated here are meant to *replace* the market. This clearly has a major role to play in broadcasting and one that will undoubtedly grow as a result of the new technology. But there is nothing whatsoever inevitable about the form that the market will take. Still more important, the unrestrained market will not produce the broadcasting that is desirable. For this we need a thoughtfully designed broadcasting policy in which the public and private and the global and local sectors complement one another. The UK has in the past managed to do this rather well. There is no reason—apart from a lack of will or thought—why we should not repeat the success in the future.

Biographical Note

Andrew Graham is the Acting Master of Balliol College, and a distinguished economist with practical experience of government at the centre.

Notes

1 Dermot Nolan, Convergent Decisions Group, paper at the LBS Conference on The Economics and Regulation of Pay Broadcasting, 10 January 1997.
2 Michael Bacharach, 'Commodities, language and desire', *Journal of Philosophy*, Vol. 87, pp. 346–68, 1990.
3 A more extensive version of these arguments can be found in Andrew Graham and Gavyn Davies, *Broadcasting, Society and Policy in the Multimedia Age*, London, John Libbey, 1997.
4 *Television Requires Responsibility*, Bertelsmann Foundation, Germany, Guetersloh, 1995.

Are the Broadsheets becoming Unhinged?

COLIN SEYMOUR-URE

UNTIL 1997 Labour had never enjoyed the majority support of the national press in a general election. It was clear at the time that this seismic shift was the start of a negotiation with a new government and a split Conservative Party rather than a firm commitment to Labour. Now that the election can be viewed in perspective, is there a case for saying that what happened is that the quality (or broadsheet) press, in particular, has become unhinged? If so, what are the implications, do they matter, and what might be done about them?

The usefulness of an 'unhinged' image is that it goes beyond the idea of detachment—in this case, from the Conservative Party—to evoke wilder visions of derangement. Instead of swinging from one side of the party system to another, papers are losing their fixed attachments in politics, or so one may claim. They are likely to become increasingly changeable, unpredictable, expediential, inconsistent. The 1997 General Election was simply an intense political moment in a process that has been continuing for some time.

This claim can best be illustrated by analysing *the decline of the single editorial voice*. In the historic model, the leading article, or editorial, was the definitive corporate statement of a paper's opinions, anonymous and, through the editorial 'we', magisterial. *The Times* was 'the Thunderer' in its Victorian heyday. Trollope could put it in his novels as *The Jupiter* and call its editor one of the two most powerful men in the land, not because of its dominant market position, but because of its editorials. Well into the Murdoch era, *The Times* thought of itself as the Thunderer when in self-congratulatory mood. Its bicentennial anthology in 1985 was titled, awkwardly, *We Thundered Out* (Times Books, 1985).

If *The Times* was the extreme case, the same was true to some degree for papers in general, and it has remained true. Even the mass market tabloids (the *Sun, Mirror* and *Daily Star*) routinely have editorials, though some are very short. The *Sun* (56) had rather more than *The Times* (49) in the six weeks up to polling day in 1997. It may well be that papers value them more than their readers do. At the same time as providing readers with a guide to news priorities and tone throughout the paper, they are a benchmark for the staff themselves: a daily exercise in updating and redrafting what a manager might nowadays wincingly call the paper's mission statement. Consistent with this status, the editorial has often been set in distinctive type or wide columns, or enclosed in a box, or surmounted by an emblem: signals, all of them, that readers should realise that the article is special.

© The Political Quarterly Publishing Co. Ltd. 1998
Published by Blackwell Publishers, 108 Cowley Road, Oxford OX4 1JF, UK and 350 Main Street, Malden, MA 02148, USA

Decline of the Editorial Voice

In recent years, however, the editorial has been becoming less special. The earliest sign was the personalisation of broadsheet writing. Anonymity had been a force for consistency and collectivity, an affirmation that facts and arguments mattered regardless of their authorship. Geoffrey Dawson, near-sovereign editor of *The Times* for all but a few years between 1912 and 1941, was irritated by specialist correspondents such as the military strategist B. H. Liddell Hart, who 'spatchcocked' personal opinions into their articles and were 'viewy'. With the regular exception (and conceit) of 'Oliver Edwards', the pseudonym under which the editor William Haley wrote a weekly book column, *The Times* had few if any bylines until Roy Thomson became owner in 1967.

Personality journalism meant that writers could be valued, not for what they wrote, but who they were. Columnists could be *prima donnas*, as they had been for decades in the popular dailies. Editors started to become public figures. Contrast, for instance, the rather private *persona* of Dennis Hamilton, who presided over the growth of the *Sunday Times* in the late 1950s and 1960s, with the flamboyance of his recent successor Andrew Neil. Neil was to a considerable extent editor-as-publicist, combining a vigorous broadcasting career with his editorial duties. The expansion of current affairs broadcasting, of course, gave a major impetus to personality journalism from the 1960s onwards. Contracts of *Times* journalists in the anonymous days did not normally permit them to broadcast; and they could hardly have broadcast anonymously anyway.

The proliferation of named columnists in the broadsheet papers needs no more than illustration here.[1] When the *Independent* was founded in 1986, a significant selling point was the recruitment from *The Times*, then at a low ebb, of staff including high profile columnists such as Peter Jenkins. The *Guardian* uses a variety of columnists. There are even spoof columnists, such as the *Guardian*'s Bel Littlejohn and 'Peter Bradshaw's Alan Clark's Diary' in the *Evening Standard*. The latter so provoked the real Alan Clark, currently MP for Kensington and Chelsea, that he sued for libel—successfully. Part of the renaissance of the *Daily Telegraph* in the late 1980s was a brightening of the leader pages with columnists. At the start of the 1997 election campaign, the *Telegraph* presented its election 'Comment team', containing altogether nine regular columnists. These were to be augmented by 'an array of guest writers', including a daily 'Alternative Voice' from the left-wing playwright David Hare ('always controversial'). In addition, there were three colour writers on the party battle buses, to 'catch the mood of the campaign with wit and style', and 'analysts' such as Professor Anthony King.

The exact boundaries between comment, mood-catching and analysis were not in practice particularly clear; but altogether, the team amounted to a large number of voices. Comparable teams wrote, obviously, in the other broadsheets. Notable among them were ex-editors. In the *Daily Telegraph*, there was Bill Deedes, editor until 1986. In the *Guardian*, there was Peter Preston; in the *Sunday Times* Andrew Neil. In *The Times* there were two: William Rees-Mogg and Simon Jenkins. A further twist was that at least three editors wrote opinion columns in their own names from time to time, as well as writing anonymous editorials. These were Charles Moore (*Daily Telegraph*), Andrew Marr (*Independent*) and Will Hutton (*Observer*).

In addition to active ex-editors, there is a small category of what might be termed editorial superiors. Hugo Young, *Guardian* columnist, is also chairman of the Scott Trust, which owns the Guardian titles (including the *Observer* and *Manchester Evening News*). This does not make him editor-in-chief, but it is difficult to believe it does not affect his relationship with the editor for whom he writes. Andrew Knight, at the Murdoch papers, and Sir David English at the *Daily Mail* group have also had super-editor roles.

In the latter cases, these roles have evidently included being an intermediary between editors and the proprietor. Such certainties as existed since 1945 about the role of proprietors did not survive beyond, say, the mid-1980s. Until then, from the reader's perspective, proprietors either had an involvement which was well known or they were penumbral figures barely glimpsed beneath the ermine. Thus Lord Beaverbrook was famous as a former cabinet minister, who claimed (somewhat speciously) to run his papers solely for the purpose of propaganda. The Astors made plain that they owned *The Times*, but did not determine editorial policy (nor, one of his cousins teased Lord Astor of Hever, actually read it). Lord Hartwell's role at the *Telegraph* titles might be obscure, but readers had no doubt the papers were as nearly 'official' Conservative organs as one could find. The *Independent* was so called specifically because nobody (at first) was allowed to own more than ten per cent of the shares. It was to be in no one's pocket.

Proprietors seem to have become more visible for two reasons. One is a matter of temperament. Roy Thomson liked to follow the Astors' example when he took over *The Times*, but Rupert Murdoch is widely known to influence his papers' opinions, even if the nature of that influence is not in the academic sense researchable. Conrad Black has been a more visible proprietor of the *Telegraph* titles than Lord Hartwell. He has, slightly bizarrely, taken part in correspondence in the *Daily Telegraph*'s letters column. He is married to one of the paper's columnists. The present Lord Rothermere did a little dance of seven veils in the months before the 1997 election, allowing Sir David English to tease *Spectator* readers, for example, with the speculation that his Lordship could even see circumstances in which the *Mail* papers might support Labour. After the election, Rothermere let it be known he would be sitting on the Labour benches in the House of Lords (though he gave no undertakings about how often he would turn up). Lord Hollick, Labour supporter since the age of fifteen and controller of the *Express* titles since 1996, let it be known he would not call the paper's tune. In May he became a part-time adviser to Trade Secretary Margaret Beckett, thereby getting closer than probably any other press baron since 1945 to actually holding government office.

Ownership and the Editorial Voice

The second reason for proprietorial visibility is structural. The entire national press belongs to multimedia conglomerates. Proprietors feature in big stories on the news and city pages and are objects of curiosity in diary columns. Predatory, they buy and sell bits of each other's empires, constantly jockeying for position in a fast-changing industry whose social, economic and technical boundaries are in permanent flux. Moreover, their industry is inescapably a matter of public policy. Gone are the days when governments could pretend that a free press meant a press free from government intervention and could leave it alone for purposes at least of direct policy, as distinct from fiscal or industrial relations. More than ever before, proprietors now have a direct vested interest in the activities of the governments and parties about which their journalists write. Small wonder if the spotlight shines on them.

Two structural changes of a different kind, lastly, have helped to blur the clarity of the traditional editorial voice. One is the competitive disadvantage of newspapers compared with broadcast media in pure news coverage: pure in the sense of unqualified by interpretation. When the *Independent* was redesigned in 1997, the editor, Andrew Marr, stressed that the style reflected the fact that often nowadays news 'takes second place to analysis'. That being so, a single editorial voice becomes incongruous.

The second change is epitomised in a *Sunday Times* advertising slogan: 'The *Sunday Times* IS the Sunday papers'. The trend to specialised sections means that the main editorial pages have competition from comment elsewhere in the paper. This tendency began before papers separated sections out physically, as the broadsheets all do now. But sectionalisation has accentuated it.

What does all this amount to? Plainly, some of the tendencies which have reduced the clarity of the editorial voice apply not only to the broadsheets. But it is these, with deeper roots in the journalism of rationality and argument than the tabloids, for which the implications are greatest. Writing as a named columnist puts a new premium in the broadsheets upon individuality and distinctiveness. (Two of the early columnists brought into the Thomson *Times* were Auberon Waugh and Bernard Levin, each of whom had a highly individual voice.) Following from this, it is safe to claim that ex-editors can and do use their signed columns to argue against editorial lines with which they had personally disagreed when editor. Again, it is common for named columnists to work also as anonymous specialist leader writers, and it will not be surprising if they keep their best performances for their bylined articles.

The behaviour of some editors in the election campaign suggested a slight lack of confidence that could be a corollary of the numerous voices around them. As it happened, there was an exceptional turnover of national newspaper editors between the 1992 and 1997 elections. Five of the ten national daily editors in 1997 had been in post for about two years or less, and only one (Richard Lambert of the *Financial Times*) was appointed before 1992. The average age was forty-three. Of the nine Sunday editors, the average tenure was nineteen months. In the 1992 campaign, by contrast, three heavyweights, Peter Preston of the *Guardian*, Sir David English of the *Daily Mail* and Kelvin MacKenzie of the *Sun*, had an average of sixteen years in post. Even if it is wrong to infer that those editors who stepped out of the editorial chair in 1997 in order to publish their views in a signed column did so from uncertainty about asserting themselves in an editorial, readers can be excused any confusion of their own about the editorial sense of direction. Again, Andrew Marr's published diary of the 1997 election, as viewed from the chair of the *Independent*, implies a surprising lack of confidence at the moment of deciding the paper's preferred outcome. 'We won't tell our readers how to vote', Marr explains, 'because that is impertinent and would be something they'd rightly resent'.[2] Why ever so? *Independent* readers would not vote one way just because the paper told them to; and they would as likely resent being patronised by the supposition that they might, as to resent being told how to vote in the first place. A *Jupiter* thunders because the occasion demands it: he does not worry about charges of impertinence.

What has been developing, in sum, is a system of 'Op-Ed' pages, well illustrated in the 1997 General Election and almost certainly cheaper than pages filled by teams of reporters. Papers make a virtue out of a variety of opinion. Where they have a party tendency, they license some discordant voices. Readers know more than they used to about the background, families, personalities and specific views of editors: the preferences of old and new *Telegraph* editors, for instance, between Conservative leadership candidates. What the reader cannot tell, however, is exactly what is the relationship of the editor to his columnists and his other colleagues, to his proprietor, to his proprietor's intermediaries and to his active predecessors. Who is writing at the end of a fax machine, and who is fully engaged in the paper and its future? Correspondingly, what weight should the reader attach to the anonymous leading article? How many of that tribe had a voice in the discussions about it? Which of them actually believed it? Need anyone—even the editor—believe it much at all? Whose is the editorial voice? What is its authority? How deep and solid is the commitment to its opinions? How far do these drive its news coverage? In principle, one may visualise an editorial continuum. At one end lies the largely mythical 'sovereign editor', in command of a paper's opinions, which are encapsulated in the leading articles and set the tone throughout the paper. At the other lies a Babel, where leading articles have the outward appearance of superior authority, but in practice are one opinion among many. In the 1990s, no paper could possibly think of itself as a Thunderer: we are much nearer to Babel.

Implications of an Unhinged Press

The general implication of this Babel, as suggested at the start of the essay, is an instability of editorial opinion. This will tend to produce inconsistency. More alarmingly, perhaps, it also implies lack of a sense of political proportion. For example, papers' preoccupation with 'sleaze' in the mid-1990s, even when allowance is made for *fin de regime* fever, arguably went far beyond the scale of the intrinsic problem. Compared, say, with financial and sexual corruption in Washington and Ireland, the sins of a Hamilton and Merchant were small beer. The difficulty in such cases is the tendency of papers to confuse the newspaper with the news: the paper's own involvement becomes a criterion of the story's importance. In a sense, it was ever thus: W. H. Russell exposing conditions in the Crimea for *The Times*; H. M. Stanley locating Livingstone in the jungle for the *New York Herald*. In our own era, Francis Chichester's far from unique solo circumnavigation of the Globe achieved world-historical status in 1967, complete with quay-side royal dubbing at Greenwich, entirely as a result of *Sunday Times* hype, after the *Guardian* had decided to pull out of its low-key sponsorship when Chichester had only reached Cape Town.

It is harmless when feats such as Chichester's capture the public imagination (though the Palace had to announce an end to knighthoods for circumnavigators, when contemporaries followed in his wake). In politics, a lack of proportion is potentially more serious. It implies that a paper has lost touch with the broad streams of opinion which typically are brought together in the main political parties. Parties and newspapers have always been closely associated. They have a natural affinity. Parties need a voice, to argue policies, trumpet leaders, engage supporters, keep activists busy and fight electoral battles. Papers want news of the issues and personalities of the day. The growth of mass parties and the mass circulation press thus went hand in hand. Each claimed, in its own way, to 'represent' the citizen/voter, holding a mirror to society. The political system as a whole benefited, provided that the range of parties corresponded reasonably well to the range of newspapers supporting them.

Such correspondence has rarely existed. For most of this century, the Conservative press has been disproportionately strong, both in number of titles and size of circulation. Its loyalty to particular Conservative leaders and policies has been much less reliable. A simple measure of the deep-rooted connection between the press and the party system is the fact which made the majority press support for Labour in 1997 so extraordinary. In the fourteen general elections from 1945 to 1992 Labour only once had the support of as many as three national dailies, and normally it had only two. In 1997 it had six. During this period there was just one unqualified U-turn between the major parties, when the *Sun* switched from Labour to Conservative in 1974. If every paper had changed at every election, there could in theory have been 150 changes. The *Guardian* often vacillated between Labour and Liberal, and a few papers sometimes remained uncommitted, but these were blips compared with 1997.

If the era of reliable press partisanship is at an end and papers are indeed becoming unhinged, then a further implication is that they are open to capture by interest groups and factions. Capture by faction is unavoidable in a party press, unless a paper is controlled by the party leadership. Of this, there have been few examples in Britain. The *Daily Herald* comes close, since it was owned in its heyday (say, 1935–55) by its printers, Odhams, but with editorial policy reserved to the TUC and hence to the Labour Party. Official party papers tend to be dull, including latterly the *Daily Herald*, which died in 1964 because it failed to attract young readers and sufficient advertising. Officialdom goes against the grain of news values, with their liking for clashes and rows, the unusual and unexpected. But for the reasons sketched above, papers and parties are bound to argue about people and policies, and from time to time papers will be at odds with the leadership. One of John Major's problems in 1997 was that the remaining Conservative papers were largely captured by the Eurosceptic tendency in his party. In the early 1980s, correspondingly, a problem for Labour under Michael Foot's leadership was that such left-leaning papers as existed were warmly sympathetic to the breakaway Social Democratic Party or hostile to important parts of the official Labour policy.

'Breakaway' is a key word there. An unhinged press is more likely than a loyalist press either to lead or follow a faction out of a party altogether, to climb aboard Jimmy Goldsmith's Referendum Party bandwagon, for instance. As it was, of course, Goldsmith had to buy his press coverage in the form of advertisements, on which he spent £6.8 million, compared with the Conservatives' £2.3 million and Labour's £1.5 million. He also distributed at least five million copies of the party's video.[3] Papers may alternatively follow the star of interest groups which are not integrated into parties at all. This need not be a consistent commitment, say, to environmentalism, decriminalisation of drugs, republicanism, animal rights or any other item of the changing agenda offered by well-organised interests. Rather, the lack of a guiding party star frees papers to wander down any alluring path. Party conviction makes the whole greater than the sum of the parts. Interest group support, by comparison, means an accumulation of mere enthusiasms with no certainty of overall coherence. The guiding star may be economy: interest groups, increasingly, do the research and a paper need not undertake expensive investigative journalism. Or the star may be circulation and a *Sun*-style populism pandering to readers' known prejudices.

The final implication of an unhinged press is that it accentuates the potential of media as a political constituency in their own right. While politics and journalism have always been entwined careers, the route to leadership and government office has lain almost entirely through fairly long party and parliamentary service. Lloyd George sought to build himself a political base after the collapse of the First World War coalition by purchase of a national newspaper (including an attempt to buy *The Times*, after Northcliffe's death in 1922); but he was already an ex-Prime Minister, leading a faction of the Liberal Party, and his case is exceptional. An unhinged press is far more open now to the possibility of use as a constituency, more or less separate from party, on which to construct a bid for office. The fact that papers are part of multimedia conglomerates greatly increases the scope. Suppose Elton John had decided to run with the Referendum Party idea (a candle in the wind?); or that David Dimbleby fancied a go at politics. The combined launching power of football clubs, pop music, TV, newspapers and marketing firms was used by Berlusconi. He swept to power as Prime Minister of Italy after just a three-month campaign leading up to the 1994 elections. It is presumably the international nature of their enterprises which prevents Britain's media moguls contemplating political careers in the manner of such predecessors as Northcliffe, Rothermere, Beaverbrook, Bracken and even Reith, but there is nothing to prevent them throwing their weight behind a *protégé*. Minor league media moguls, among whom Richard Branson may be counted, are perhaps more likely to be tempted. Branson's assiduous self-publicity, epitomised in his ballooning escapades, have got him talked of as a candidate for the post of London's new Mayor (regardless of how seriously he himself may actually take the possibility).

An Unhinged Press: Should We Worry?

An unhinged press, in short, will help destabilise the British party system. Interest groups and parties work against one another. In the textbook truism, groups stress particular interests, parties the general interest. Papers speaking in a multitude of voices better reflect the politics of an interest group culture than do party papers. This is the best argument for saying that it does not matter if the press is unhinged. One can make an increasingly strong case that the political party in its familiar form during the last half-century of predominantly two-party competition has had its day. Most of the things parties have conventionally done are now done more effectively by other organisations, chiefly by interest groups, but also think tanks, universities and media. Groups define and articulate problems requiring political action. They invite membership and participation. They are at least as good at raising money as parties. Their resources often enable them to do much better policy research than can parties in traditional party preserves such as social, economic, defence and education policy. They can make themselves heard in Parliament, increasingly via the system of specialised and departmental select committees (which themselves have captured much of the attention formerly concentrated on the generalist arena of the House of Commons chamber). They provide an alternative to parties as launching pads for a career in parliamentary politics. They have advantages over parties in the promotion and marketing of policies, whether as 'insider groups' with access to civil servants irrespective of the party in power, or as 'outsider groups' exploiting the media in the politics of protest and direct action.

Party's sole remaining advantages over interest groups probably lie in the geographical representation of citizens in Parliament and—by far the more important—in monopolising the pool of talent from which ministers are drawn. Hence parties are at their richest, most populous, most energised and most effective during the frenetic few weeks of each general election campaign. Once in office, however, governments are surely involved in the game of pressure politics now more than ever before, not least because their backbench supporters are involved in it too.

On this argument, then, there is nothing to worry about: the unhinging of the press simply reflects, part as cause, part as effect, the organic development of the body politic as a system responding to patterns of interest group behaviour more than to parties. Alternatively, there may be nothing to worry about if the initial analysis of the essay is wrong and the unhinging of the press proves a short-term phenomenon. Despite the factors causing a decline in the single editorial voice, papers might regain a singleness of political purpose if the Conservative Party restored its unity, especially over Europe, and reestablished effective leadership. Meanwhile, the party's own uncertainties are simply echoed in the detachment of the press, and the press itself usurps the role of parliamentary Opposition. Ministers and spin doctors fight the Government's case in signed contributions to features and letters pages and in bruising encounters on Radio 4 and TV current affairs programmes, without needing to worry about winning points in Parliament.

On other grounds, however, an unhinged press remains worrying. First, the selfish centrifugal forces of interest group politics are intrinsically divisive and unequal. They need countering even (perhaps especially) at a time when the physical and political boundaries of the nation state are in question, both supranationally and through devolution. Media have a capacity to bind people together. The common ground sought by parties is represented in the daily newspaper. Despite sectionalisation, it remains a product of *general* interest: the technical is treated in non-technical terms. Sectionalisation is in fact a means of incorporating special-interest material within a general-interest package. If party politics is yielding to interest group politics, then papers are well placed to act as a counterforce. With their broad perspective, they can resist the runaway popular appeal of ephemeral and eccentric ideas and persons. Any tendency to populism in the broadsheets would be profoundly depressing, for this reason if no other. There is populism enough and to spare in the tabloids.

An unhinged press, secondly, tends to create a *laager* mentality in parties (particularly the government party). The *Guardian* clearly regards itself as the Blair Government's candid friend. This is not how Downing Street sees it, to judge by the hostile reactions to some of its coverage. Parties need at least some opportunities to present themselves as they wish (misguidedly or not) to be seen. Failure to enable this is a failure of the democratic process. Within the range of op-ed voices in a contemporary broadsheet, there is room for government voices. But this does not necessarily carry conviction with partisans about the principles governing news coverage.

For much of the post-1945 period the pat answer to complaints about press bias was that the broadcasting organisations are legally required to be scrupulously fair. Yet at exactly the time when the press is becoming unhinged, this non-partisanship is at risk. The broadcasters' traditional benchmark of balance and fairness has been party representation in Parliament. As the two major parties' share of votes and seats has declined, this has become less satisfactory even as a quantitative measure. As a qualitative guide to what topics should be treated, how this should be done and by whom, it has always been useless. Throughout the last thirty years, broadcasters have exercised their own judgment in these matters with more and more discretion. Instead of slavishly following the parties' agenda in election campaigns, for instance, they have decided their own. The growth in TV and radio channels and broadcasting hours has compounded the trend enormously in recent years. No longer can politicians assume that at least in the broadcast media they will be presented largely as they wish to be seen. On the contrary, spin doctoring has flourished to a great extent precisely because they cannot. In the extreme case of Northern Ireland, the Thatcher Government removed broadcasters' discretion altogether, by using statutory powers to ban the voices of extremists from the airwaves completely. (The ban lasted from 1988 to 1994.) In everyday politics, however, party managers have to use informal methods in the unending struggle to keep the right people on and off the air, talking to the right interviewers and saying the right things. The *laager* mentality thrives. Meanwhile, interest group leaders use their own media skills to get a public hearing. Broadcasters avoid editorialising as scrupulously as ever. But the public service broadcasting ethic positively encourages diversity of access; and while the broadcast agenda can be deliberately non-partisan it can never avoid having political implications. Broadcast media are of decreasing help, therefore, as a counterbalance to an unhinged press.

One last reason for concern about an unhinged press is the implication for press accountability. When Baldwin attacked Rothermere and Beaverbrook for seeking 'power without responsibility', this was the concern he had in mind. Editors claim readers as a franchise, juts as politicians claim voters. If either lose the confidence of their mass base, their legitimacy fails. But readers need to be clear about where their paper stands, as do voters with their party. If readers are uninterested (as very many are, who do not buy a paper for its politics), that is all the more reason, arguably, why the paper should be firmly linked, if only by conviction, to an external organisation or set of values which does have popular endorsement.

Countering the Effects of an Unhinged Press

What might be done to mitigate the effects of an unhinged press? To the extent that the development reflects the growth of an interest group political culture, not much can be expected. One practical palliative is to take up the cry with which S. E. Finer ended his book *Anonymous Empire*, the first study of British pressure groups (London, Pall Mall Press, 1958): 'Light! More light!' First, the newspaper proprietors should be flushed out. In a world where every lightbulb has a mission statement, they should be obliged to place on record a statement about their paper's political principles and the internal procedures through which these are decided and applied, including the role of the proprietor himself. (Northcliffe did indeed include a mission statement in the first number of the *Daily Mail* in 1896, a short paragraph headed 'THE EXPLANATION'.) These statements would, of course, be anodyne, but they need not be vacuous. They would have some of the limitations of the 'voluntary code' method of self-regulation (e.g. for professional ethics, invasion of privacy and so on). But these limitations do not make such codes entirely useless. They are a benchmark and a hostage to fortune. A paper's mission statement should form part of the company's annual report, which should also include a review of the paper's editorial stance during the previous year. Statement and review should be published in the paper. Beyond that, proprietors should be encouraged to talk and write more openly about their involvement in their papers. It should be publicly unacceptable for a proprietor such as Lord Hollick to act even as a part-time adviser to ministers without going on the record about his relation to his newspapers.

Lord Hollick very likely has gone on the record. Part of the 'Light! More light!' difficulty is that, since the reform of the old Press Council, there is nowhere obvious to discover such information about newspapers. About broadcasting, there never has been, since the BBC monopoly ended. The Department of Culture, Media and Sport ought to establish a Media Register (or contract out the job). Its focus would be principally upon ownership and control. Its purpose would be to track and record movement in the ownership of media companies of all kinds, and to draw attention to matters of public interest. The latter could include cross-ownership, foreign ownership, the commercial operations of the BBC, trends in concentration, conglomeration, regional patterns, and so on. The register would not be concerned with media performance. At present such tracking is wholly haphazard. Or does the Department do it? If so, the work should certainly be in the public domain.

Even to describe such a register in little more than a grunt is to draw attention again to the significance of newspapers as a policy field. In an interest group culture, media organisations *are* interest groups. Unlike other groups, they both participate in the political process and evaluate it. The more they are participants, the more important it is that their readers understand the factors influencing their role as evaluators. In the endless dance of government, press and people, the roles of oppressor, victim and guardian change. Sometimes, as with privacy, government threatens to intervene, so as to curb newspaper excess. At other times, as with 'sleaze', newspapers expose corruption in government. The political unhinging of the broadsheet papers, and the decline of the single editorial voice, are a weakness in the press and ultimately in the political system.

Biographical Note

Colin Seymour-Ure is Professor of Government at Kent University. His first book on the media and politics was *The Press Politics and the Public*, and his most recent, *The British Press and Broadcasting since 1945*, was published in 1996.

Notes

1 An entertaining and original analysis of the recent development of columnists is in Jeremy Tunstall, *Newspaper Power*, Oxford, Clarendon Press, 1996, ch. 17.
2 The diary, titled 'The night we nearly ran out of paper', is in *British Journalism Review*, Vol. 8, No. 2, 1997, pp. 7–14.
3 This staggering figure is quoted in David Butler and Dennis Kavanagh, *The British General Election of 1997*, London, Macmillan, 1997, p. 219. The pollster MORI found 22 per cent of households claiming to have received the video.

Scottish Devolution and the Media

PHILIP SCHLESINGER

THIS chapter considers the relationships between constitutional change, the news media, and the reshaping of political and communicative boundaries in the United Kingdom. We need to think again about these spaces because they are being reshaped from above and from below. The first source of pressure is the ineluctable march of the European Union into the heartlands of political life. The second is the imminent impact on the British state of an autonomous, national, Scottish polity, the first major step in a wider process of constitutional reform. Although the EU provides the wider framework for this discussion, the devolution of powers to a new Scottish parliament is my principal focus here. This is already propelling questions of media policy onto the public agenda in Scotland and provoking the development of a new political culture.

Political communication and the nation-state

Political communication—the purposive communication by political actors about public affairs—conventionally takes the nation-state as its framework. In everyday political life it is still generally assumed that the United Kingdom is a bounded, sovereign polity, with its own national political agenda, communicated by its own national media. This dominant view of the relations between national political space and national communicative space is still supported by a well-established perspective in the theory of nationalism, which needs to be revised, and is beginning to be so.

Consider the line of work represented by, successively, Karl Deutsch, Ernest Gellner, Benedict Anderson, and more recently Michael Billig.[1] All share a broad concern with how nations speak to themselves, how they mark themselves off, or flag themselves, as different from others. All theorise from within what Deutsch first labelled a 'social communications' perspective whose axial premise is that nations are set apart from other collectivities because of the special nature of their internal communications. Consequently, it is held that a given cultural collectivity tends to build up and secure a separate national identity over time. While each theorist may differ as to the key explanatory factor, it is commonly argued that educational systems, the media, standardised languages or shared cultural practices and symbols are key elements in the historical process of national-culture building. Such national cultures and resultant identities are assumed to be both politically underpinned and continually developed by a state.

This underlying assumption has also been shared by the critical theorist

Jürgen Habermas, whose influential theory of communication initially took as its framework the *nation* addressed as a political community. Political communication within the nation need not necessarily take a *democratic* form. However, in Habermas' theory, and in the work of the many scholars who have tried to develop it further in recent years, it is precisely how to ensure access to communicative power by citizens that has become a central concern.[2]

Much current discussion has centred on the so-called 'public sphere', a term promoted in academic discourse through the English translation of Habermas's work, and now in relatively wide use. This refers to the domain of debate that exists outside the state, but which is centred on the state's activities and engages all who are concerned with matters of public interest. This is the space of civil society, where political parties, voluntary associations and organised interests may intervene in the political process. The existence of such a domain—in which the media are also situated—is central to the freedom of expression commonly associated with democracy. Thus conceived, the public sphere presupposes a nation-state in relation to which civil society can think and organise politically.

The public sphere is therefore commonly seen as co-extensive with the political form of *nation-statehood*. This view has a bearing on the present-day functioning of political communication in the United Kingdom, because in reality the dominant model of the nation-state as a unitary political community, as a stable locus in which we speak to ourselves about politics and public affairs, is breaking down.

Symptomatic is the persistent line of media commentary on the difficulties of defining 'Britishness'. An important, and highly visible, part of the Blair Government's politics has been the effort to 'rebrand' the United Kingdom and give it a new identity. The discourse of modernised Britishness is the happy hunting-ground of the think-tank intelligentsia. In 1997, the political annexation of the sentiments generated by the death of Diana, Princess of Wales (apparently, for some, a rediscovery of Britain's lost capacity for feeling), the selling of 'cool Britannia', the enforced quasi-modernisation of the monarchy, the aspirations for an undefined grandeur embodied in the New Millennium Experience, all betokened attempts to grapple with a deep-seated problem of collective identity.

As devolution in Scotland and Wales becomes imminent, and as 'Britain' and 'Britishness' start to disaggregate, the attempts to characterise 'Englishness' are gathering pace. Whether the first-term programme of New Labour constitutional reform—with elections taking place under PR systems, proposed Freedom of Information legislation, the incorporation of the European Convention on Human Rights into UK law, the intended abolition of hereditary peers, and an elected mayor for London—will result in a more *united* kingdom remains to be seen. As a modernising programme it is certainly intended to result in a new cohesion of the state, but conceivably it could provoke gradual disintegration.

The communicative challenge of 'Europeanisation'

We can less and less sensibly think of the UK as a sovereign political and communicative space, because issues arise, and agendas appear, that derive from the broader political domain of the European Union, and these cannot simply be screened out. The compelling question of Britain's position on European Monetary Union (EMU) is the prime illustration of this. By opting to delay entry to the European single currency, the British government has in effect placed itself on the sidelines. On this decision hangs the future economic performance of the UK as well as the British state's political influence. A telling, if less fundamental example, has been the EU's key role in repeatedly deciding the terms of trade and outcomes of the Bovine Spongiform Encephalopathy (BSE) crisis.

The British practice of politics has been steadily 'Europeanised' as Westminster has ceased to be the sole arbiter of decision-making. Moreover, increasingly, the question of Britain's approach to European integration has the capacity to make and break political parties. After all, long-standing internal divisions over 'Europe' had a decisive role in shattering the long Conservative hold over the country both before, and during, the General Election of 1997.

The increasing centrality of European integration for the future of British politics deeply affects how we should think about the nation-state as a locus of political communication, in which journalism plays a key role alongside the promotional activities of a range of political actors including state agencies, parties, and pressure groups. As debates about major European policy issues routinely occur in the domestic heartlands of the polity, and are manifestly central to the agendas of British news media, the lines between 'us' (the British) and 'them' (the Continentals) are becoming increasingly blurred.

So while, routinely, the EU may be represented as external to the British political system, in reality it is increasingly *internal* to it. The often distance-taking political rhetoric and prevalently negative media coverage obscure this fact. However, these are surface reactions to a deeper movement. It is hard to see clearly the real, underlying extent of the current change in politico-communicative boundaries precisely because the way the highly complex relationship between the EU and the UK is handled both politically and in news coverage varies from moment to moment. Two brief illustrations from my research in progress on contemporary political communication support this view.[3]

In May 1996, for example, the volume of radio and television coverage of a number of European stories (notably reconsideration by the EU of the export ban on British beef) showed a marked increase over previous months. Moreover, the range of political figures given access to the airwaves significantly increased, with sources from several EU member states playing a major role in British debate. At the time, a matter of major UK national interest was being decided *not* at Westminster, but in Brussels. Irrespective of the arguments, it was evident that the UK's broadcast forums of political argument and reporting had opened up to include the EU's spokespeople. In a marked shift, then, the EU's political space for a moment directly overlapped with the UK's, becoming an integral part of British communicative space.

Although such moments of relative openness occur, there may also be a countervailing tendency to closure, illustrated during the British General Election campaign of 1997. On 21 April, Jacques Santer, President of the European Commission, intervened with a swinging attack on 'Euro-sceptics'. General Election campaigns are moments of national self-enclosure, when domestic concerns swell in importance and completely dominate political debate and media agendas. The polity could hardly be more self-absorbed at such times, so Santer's attack on the Euro-sceptics, coupled with his uncompromising federalist agenda, played directly into the British political battlefield. Both the political class, and the press, were largely unanimous about putting Jacques back in his box, with some chauvinistic insults thrown in for good measure. For the Conservative Prime Minister, John Major, this was a chance to defend the British national interest and reassert his anti-federalism, whereas for the Labour aspirant, Tony Blair, it was a moment to blow the patriotic trumpet and reaffirm his gold-plated Britishness. On this occasion the EU, through the symbolic figure of the Commission's President, could easily be represented as alien and intrusive, even dictatorial, and the speech as a gross interference in domestic politics, as an affront to national sovereignty.

Such divergent instances suggest that both the political debate and media reporting of the EU in Britain may shift along a continuum of relative openness and closure to European perspectives and arguments. However, the introjection of European matters into British political and communicative space is undeniable and not as just *another* story, but rather as one integral to the secular melting-down of EU member states' boundaries. European integration is beginning to have an unevenly distributed impact both on conceptions of citizenship and of collective belonging. After all, since the 1991 Treaty of Union (signed at Maastricht), the category of EU citizenship *has* existed alongside established national citizenship, and although its precise implications have been a matter of debate, it has introduced a new layer of complexity and of potential loyalty. This may, in time, produce another form of collective identity—'Europeanness'—for the citizens of member states.

Political theory is beginning to catch up with the realities on the ground. Indicatively, in his more recent work, Jürgen Habermas has written of the European Union as itself constituting a complex public sphere, where the historic nation-states articulate with an emergent federal one—a viewpoint, incidentally, that neglects the place of stateless nations. If such a new European polity is indeed emerging, it is still embryonic. However, this rethinking of political space transforms the conventional role of political communication as a vehicle for addressing a nation-state-centred public and compels us to consider its relation to a putative *supranational* public.[4] The corollary of the enlargement of the public sphere is that a European civil society must eventually emerge, the nucleus of which already exists in the policy communities clustered around the EU's executive and legislative institutions.

We might now, in retrospect, re-read almost two decades of tortured debates in the EU about the role of the media in helping to build variously a common culture, or an information society, or a democratic public, and in reflecting the Union's developing impact on the communicative spaces still jealously guarded by the member states. This effect is likely to increase as European Monetary Union impels greater de facto federalisation and as communication policy frameworks established in Brussels increasingly constrain member states.[5]

Scotland's quiet 'democratic revolution'

If 'Europeanisation' is by stages redefining the space of political communication in Britain, so too is the current internal reshaping of the state due to the devolution of power to Scotland and Wales. Decentralisation is a widespread feature of contemporary politics in most EU member states, and the UK is finally aligning itself with the European trend towards 'subsidiarity', the doctrine that no political issue should be decided at a level higher than is absolutely necessary.[6] The New Labour victory on 1 May 1997 placed home rule for the two countries firmly back on the British political agenda after almost two decades, initiating what constitutional reformers such as Anthony Barnett see as a 'democratic revolution'. Constitutional change is truly fundamental, as Barnett notes, because it embodies 'the set of relationships that proposes how a country is run', and therefore profoundly affects the institutional core of a society and how people live their everyday lives.[7]

In Scotland, the government published its devolution White Paper, *Scotland's Parliament*, in July 1997, a moment of restrained triumph for the Secretary of State for Scotland, Donald Dewar.[8] This was rapidly followed by a two-question referendum on 11 September 1997 in which voters were asked to decide whether there should be a Scottish Parliament and whether this body should have the power to vary taxation. A telling majority of Scots voted for political autonomy. After the devastation of the Conservatives in the May election, there was little serious opposition from those in favour of the centralist status quo. The 'Yes-Yes' campaign unprecedently brought together Scotland's two main devolutionist parties, Labour and the Liberal-Democrats, with the pro-independence Scottish National Party (SNP). The referendum implicitly identified the Scots as a civic nation, as voting was open only to residents of Scotland, irrespective of other ethnic backgrounds or places of birth. Ethnic Scots outside the country had no voting rights. This is an important benchmark, though still little appreciated, for future political discourse about 'the nation' in Scotland.

On a turn-out of 60.4 per cent, in response to the first question, 74.3 per cent supported the creation of a Scottish Parliament, while, in response to the second, 63.5 per cent agreed that the proposed legislature should have tax-varying powers. The 1997 vote was a milestone, as it turned around the result of the previous referendum of 1979. Support for a Scottish Parliament with wide powers, within the United Kingdom, finally addressed the 'unfinished business' of constitutional reform, expressing 'the settled will of the Scottish people', in the two resonant phrases of the late Labour Party leader and convinced devolutionist, John Smith. Any future choice will now be between remaining in the Union and outright independence.

The extensive pro-devolutionary shift during the Conservative years did not come out of the blue. The Tories had become steadily more beleaguered north of the Border. By the 1992 General Election, the Conservatives had been returned in only 11 of the 72 Scottish seats. 1997 was a turning-point for them, as they lost all their Scottish seats. The disjuncture between increasingly unpopular Conservative rule from Westminster and the small Tory representation in Scotland had contributed to a widespread sense of disenfranchisement over the years. The various campaigns waged against devolution after 1992 by John Major and his successive Scottish Secretaries Ian Lang and Michael Forsyth thus proved to be ineffective in saving the party from electoral collapse in 1997.

Much of the groundwork for the July 1997 White Paper and subsequent Bill was prepared through the patient work of the Scottish Constitutional Convention, which first met in March 1989. Little known outside Scotland, this has been a crucial vehicle for key elements of Scottish civil society to devise a common approach to devolution. Contributing to the Convention's initial impetus was a resentment of the strident centralism of Margaret Thatcher. This had led to the widespread sense that Scotland was not adequately represented by Westminster politics. The Convention brought together Scotland's dominant Labour Party and the Liberal Democrats, also including other minor parties and representatives of a wide range of interests, such as the Scottish Trades Union Congress (STUC), the women's movement, local councils, and the churches. The core of its political project was the restoration of Home Rule to Scotland within the framework of the United Kingdom. Both the anti-devolution Conservatives and the independence-oriented SNP refused to join.[9]

To legitimise its opposition to the constitutional status quo, the Convention invoked the will of the Scottish nation. By seeing sovereignty as vested in 'the people' rather than in the Crown-in-Parliament at Westminster, it drew a sharp distinction between Scottish and English constitutional thinking. The Convention also pointed to decentralising developments in the European Union to bolster its intellectual case. As an expression of civil society, it could draw both on the legacy of the Scottish Enlightenment and find inspiration in civic movements intent on promoting political change and democratisation in East-Central Europe. Crucially, the work of the Constitutional Convention was coupled with the largely supportive agenda-setting role amongst the 'blethering classes' of the Scottish broadsheet press, which showed a consistent interest in its activities, as did Scottish broadcasters.

The Convention managed to maintain a remarkably broad political consensus over a period of eight years. It produced a series of key documents—notably *A Claim of Right for Scotland* (1989) and *Scotland's Parliament; Scotland's Right* (1995)—which set the stage in 1997 for the eventual White Paper, *Scotland's Parliament* (July) and the subsequent historic Scotland Bill (December), whose provisions are very far-reaching.[10]

Devolution means that Scotland will legislate in all major areas except those reserved to Westminster which are principally the constitution, UK financial matters, foreign policy, defence, social security and citizenship. Given our present concern with communication, it is crucial to note that powers over broadcasting have been reserved to Westminster. Powers in Scotland will encompass key areas such as health, education, local government, economic development and transport, environment, agriculture, forestry and fishing, law and home affairs, sport and the arts, and permit a tax-varying power of up to 3 per cent of basic income tax.

The first general election will be in May 1999. There will initially be 129 Members of the Scottish Parliament (MSPs), 73 elected by the first-past-the-post system in existing Westminster constituencies, with an additional member voting system electing 56 members from party lists, seven from each of the eight European parliamentary constituencies.

Scotland's press and national identity

Since the Acts of Union of 1707 (when Scotland's last parliament was dissolved), the country has retained its separate legal and educational systems and church, all of which, with differing importance over time, have contributed to the shaping of a distinct national culture. Since 1886, the national institutional matrix has also had a territorial, political and administrative dimension in the shape of the Scottish Office. The case for a parliament has latterly been made in terms of the need to extend democratic control over this bureaucratic structure.

Scotland's media are a crucial element of the country's civil society. Their role in the development of the new Scottish political culture once the parliament is established will be substantial. They are part of the range of institutions that have been the substratum of Scottish distinctiveness within the UK. It is not surprising, therefore, that Scots have the option of a dual national identity, Scottish and/or British. The current evidence suggests that Scottishness is increasingly preferred over Britishness.[11]

The creation of a Scottish Parliament is a key test bed for sociological and political analyses concerned with the 'stateless nation'. It seems that the British multi-national state is likely to experience the strains of 'asymmetrical government' if English regionalism does not take off following Scottish and

Welsh devolution.[12] Thus far, there have been some competitive regionalist stirrings in England's North-East, but how deep-rooted these are is open to question.

Unlike any other British region, for most Scots the 'national media' are based not in London, but rather 'located in Scotland, within a UK framework of ownership control, finance and regulation. The semi-autonomous state of the Scottish media thus parallels that of other features of Scottish political and economic life'. It has been argued that 'in many respects the media in Scotland have their own distinctive characteristics and can be said to contribute, particularly in the case of the press, to Scotland's self-perception as a nation'.[13]

In fact, it is unclear to what extent the self-conscious identification with Scotland of the Scottish-based press, radio and television promotes a sense of distinctive Scottishness amongst the public. While some might argue that the media do significantly shape Scottish identity, others have speculated that the distinctiveness of the Scottish media has been shaped by the pre-existing national culture.[14] Whatever the precise causal relation, for present purposes we may assume that there is an intimate reciprocal connection between the media consumption patterns of the Scottish public and Scottish national and regional identities.

In the long run-up to the 1997 General Election, devolution was a topic of exceptionally intensive and extensive media interest north of the Border, especially so when systematically compared with coverage in the London-based press and broadcasting. Subsequently, this distinctive pattern of attention has been sustained during the reporting of the devolution White Paper, the Referendum and the publication of the Scotland Bill, maintaining the south's communication deficit. It could be argued that a fracture line runs through the UK when it comes to public dissemination of the implications of Scottish devolution.

As my concern here is with political communication strictly understood, I shall limit myself to giving a brief account of some of the most significant Scottish news media, underlining how they differ from the London-based UK media. Clearly, to explore other dimensions of the relationships between media and national identity one would cast the net much more widely in the media culture, to take in mainstream broadcast sport, music, comedy, drama, talk shows, phone-ins, magazines, advertising and cinema as well as Scottish Office-supported Gaelic television production. Readership figures are a crude indicator of consumption preferences, and tell us nothing of the meanings attributed to what is read. However, they do indicate the strong hold that Scottish-produced and headquartered newspapers exercise in the country, when compared with most of those published south of the Border. Scotland has an old-established daily quality press in the shape of *The Herald* (Glasgow, founded 1783) and *The Scotsman* (Edinburgh, founded 1817). Jointly, these newspapers dominate the opinion-leading market in, respectively, West and East-Central Scotland, the belt where most of the population is concentrated. Between them, in 1996–7, these two titles reached more than 13 per cent of readers, whereas the five London broadsheets together attracted some 8 per cent.[15]

The popular end of the daily newspaper market is also extremely distinctive. It is dominated by the *Daily Record* (founded 1895, and Britain's oldest popular daily newspaper). The country's leading daily tabloid, the *Record* has a readership of some 1.8 million, a reach of 44 per cent of Scotland's adults, and is especially read in the west of the country. Its nearest rival is the *Scottish Sun*, with around a quarter of the readership. Against these front-runners, London titles such as the *Daily Mirror* or the *Daily Star* have very modest sales by the usual tabloid standards.

The middle market has recently been prone to penetration by Scottish editions of London newspapers, with both the *Scottish Daily Mail* and the *Scottish Daily Express* each building significant readerships of over a quarter of a million. However, their undeniably significant reach needs to be considered in relation to the continuing 'city state' character of Scotland's press. Mid-market tabloid circulations are matched by those of Dundee's *Courier* and Aberdeen's *Press and Journal* (founded 1798). Sunday newspaper sales are also markedly dominated by Scottish titles. The *Record*'s stable-mate, the *Sunday Mail*, reaches almost half the adult Scottish readership, with the *Sunday Post* pushing near to 40 per cent. The only southern title to come close is the *News of the World*, with virtually a quarter of Scottish readers. The quality end of the market shows the *Sunday Times* to be a close rival to *Scotland on Sunday*, each reaching some 7 per cent of readers. Unlike its southern broadsheet counterparts, however, the *Sunday Times* sold north of the Border is thoroughly Scottish in content and perspectives. The Scottish press, therefore, penetrates everyday life, and while it is certainly true that some Scottified English titles have made major inroads of late, they have had to adapt themselves to the Scottish market in order to succeed. Pressures to focus even more on national developments can only increase with the advent of the Edinburgh parliament.

The media politics of the market-place

There have been significant changes of ownership in the two quality daily newspapers, which have a disproportionately significant role in setting the agenda of Scottish affairs. In one case, that of *The Herald*, this was part of the pre-devolutionary manoeuvrings of what was to become the Scottish Media Group (SMG) in May 1997, provoking concern about media concentration, the more so after SMG brought up Grampian Television. In the other, editorial changes at *The Scotsman* have had ramifications for the debate over devolution.

In July 1996, Caledonian Newspapers, owner of *The Herald* and the Glasgow *Evening Times*, accepted a bid from Scottish Television, the ITV Central Scotland licensee. Scottish Television's executive chairman, Gus Macdonald, unashamedly played the Scottish card in a pre-election year, saying: 'I think we need a strong and robust media in Scotland and that combining the two businesses will help counter the very negative effects of power being sucked down to London'.[16]

While Scottish Television's majority ownership is in Scottish hands, 20 per cent of the company's shares are owned by the London-based Mirror Group Newspapers (MGN), which also owns the *Daily Record* and the *Sunday Mail*, two of Scotland's biggest-selling titles. Following expressions of public concern about the possibility of ownership concentration in the newspaper market, the Scottish Television-Caledonian merger was officially cleared by both the Independent Television Commission in October 1996 (applying a public interest test) and the Department of Trade and Industry (following a report from the Office of Fair Trading).

Scottish Television's other growth-point was in its home territory of television. It had long been supposed that the Glasgow-based company, broadcasting to the major Scottish central belt market, would bid for Grampian Television, headquartered in Aberdeen in Scotland's North-East. Once the provisions of the 1996 Broadcasting Act had come into effect, Grampian, which was showing improved pre-tax profits, became particularly vulnerable to take-over, as the Act allowed a single television company to reach up to 15 per cent of the entire *UK* audience. The bid came in June 1997, the month following the General Election, and was accepted by the Grampian shareholders. The proposed merger brought 4.7 of the 5.1 million Scottish viewers within SMG's purview.

Concern was expressed in various quarters about a concentration of television ownership, about job losses, and the possible loss of a regional programming identity for Grampian viewers—a touchy issue since regional politics are likely to be rather significant in the Scottish parliament. The ITC mounted an inquiry on public interest grounds and found in SMG's favour, saying that it expected the regional provisions of the two companies' separate licences to be honoured, a point recently re-emphasised by the ITC's chairman.

What was thrown into relief, and has fuelled the continuing, if still sporadic, expressions of public concern, has been the recognition that the rules designed to regulate concentration and audience share in the UK-wide market were simply not designed to take account of Scotland considered as a *political* entity, as opposed to its being regarded as a territory divided among three ITV regions. The politics of home rule are bound increasingly to underline the extent to which Scotland is a distinctive *national* market—that is, a *political* economy—in its own right.

Grampian's incorporation into SMG meant that the group now controlled some 90 per cent of the Scottish television audience for the main terrestrial commercial television channel. Only those viewers served by Border Television remained outside SMG's reach. From a UK perspective, the Scottish-Grampian merger was small beer and merely part of a flurry of government facilitated take-overs in the ITV sector that had led to three big players south of the Border. However, in a small country, a unique multimedia concentration both has a good deal of influence and considerable political visibility.

SMG pre-emptively built up its strength during the last year of Tory rule. Recognising that UK legislation dealt with Scotland as a market but not as a polity, it sought assurances that Labour, if elected, had no intention of changing this. Politicians of all stripes were willing to play the Scottish card in 1996. SMG's subsequent calculation—in line with both the White Paper and the Scotland Bill—has been that UK regulation will stay in place and that the Edinburgh parliament will have no regulatory or legislative competence in the field of broadcasting. With 80 per cent of its programmes and 85 per cent of its advertising coming though the ITV network, Scottish Television stresses its place in *British* broadcasting. Complaining that ITV was already over-regulated, Bob Tomlinson, SMG's head of public affairs, has maintained that vesting any powers in Edinburgh would be 'unwarranted, impractical and costly' and that the approach needed was 'hands off, light touch, and let us get on with the job'.[17]

Despite this call for the status quo, the advent of a Scottish parliament is likely to ensure that cross-media ownership and concentration in Scotland will remain an issue. Questions were first raised by the Broadcasting for Scotland Campaign when Caledonian Newspapers was bought, reflecting concern about an eventual take-over of Scottish Television by the Mirror Group. Criticism has more recently been clearly articulated by the SNP, which, without impugning SMG's record, has argued that it would be generally prudent to have separate 'anti-trust' laws for the media sector.

Change at *The Scotsman* has been of interest because of editorial rather than structural shifts, at least for the present. In October 1996, Andrew Neil was appointed editor-in-chief of Scotsman Publications. The company, owned by Frederick and David Barclay's European Press Holdings, groups *The Scotsman*, *Scotland on Sunday*, and the *Edinburgh Evening News*. Neil's remit also includes *The European* and *Sunday Business*.

Neil's appointment caused a stir among media commentators, given the long-standing commitment to devolution of *The Scotsman* and its Sunday stable-mate. His adamant opposition to independence and his dismissive views of what he sees as Scotland's 'monotonic' left-of-centre consensus goes back to his time at *The Sunday Times*, which consistently attacked devolution in its Scottish edition.[18] Neil's appointment, and consequent editorial changes, have certainly brought more astringent questioning to the practicalities of devolution, tempered by an acceptance that this will now indeed be the new political order. Neil summed up his mission thus in June 1997:

I had laid down that our titles must be broadly in favour of the market economy, defenders of the union between Scotland and England and prepare to tackle head on the many outdated Scottish shibboleths and collectivist attitudes which still dominate politics north of the border. None of this conflicted with backing Blair . . . [who] . . . himself told me he hoped I might be able to stir things up. . . .[19]

In the run-up to the establishment of the parliament in Edinburgh, a new phase of struggle for primacy in the quality market is underway between *The Scotsman* and *The Herald*. This is linked to the ancient rivalry between Edinburgh and Glasgow, with fears in the west of Scotland that the country's biggest city will lose out by the capital's reinforced importance. Inside *The Herald* it is recognised that *The Scotsman* has the advantage of a winning brand-name when national appeal is going to be ever more resonant. That said, the Scottish Media Group has set up a joint Edinburgh office for *The Herald* and Scottish Television, and evidently plans major coverage of the parliament.

Broadcast journalism and regulation

At the same time as building an increasingly dominant position in Scotland's media landscape, Scottish Television has also used its Scottishness to argue for more independence from the UK network, notably in news scheduling. This initiative, in Gus Macdonald's words to me, 'detonated the debate', with Scotland's other big terrestrial television player, BBC Scotland, subsequently initiating a far-reaching review.

Macdonald has argued for 'country' membership of the ITV network—in effect, for a looser, affiliate status—since late 1996. The aim is to reduce Scottish's commitment to the network, paying only for the programmes it wants. In justification, Scottish Television has claimed that it could choose to produce more programmes with high production values, such as drama and entertainment, with benefits for local audiences. Relatedly, SMG spokesmen have suggested that Scottish Television might opt out of network program-ming to cover the Edinburgh parliament and floated the idea that Scottish news delivered by the early evening flagship programme, *Scotland Today*, might be combined with UK and international stories in a 60-minute programme.[20] An early evening news that pulls together these elements now seems likely. Such a Scottish news programme would have a major impact on the broadcast media agenda north of the Border and would challenge ITN's present role in supplying identical UK-wide news to all commercial television contractors.

BBC Scotland also has to decide on the appropriate journalistic response to devolution. Even if its management wished to, it could not easily effect a semi-detached relationship to London since, like its Welsh and Northern Irish counterparts, it operates as a 'national region' within a unitary corporation. Each 'national region' has a special Broadcasting Council to act as a policy forum, and its own Controller and senior management, with lines of responsibility to London.

Although it is the only pan-Scottish terrestrial news and current affairs broadcaster, the BBC's Scottish radio and television services differ. BBC Radio Scotland is a general national station—a rarity these days—and has no single direct competitor in Scotland, although it does compete with commercial local radio. The station has had a broad remit since being launched in 1978 in anticipation of a Scottish Assembly. Created with the expectation of constitutional change in mind, its journalistic role in a devolved Scotland may be expected to be rather important, affecting radio coverage generally. Spokesmen for commercial stations have already anticipated extra expenditure on speech programming. While Radio Scotland's news and current affairs coverage has its detractors, it is nonetheless wide-ranging, and puts a distinctive Scottish slant on the stories and issues covered. Radio Scotland's *Good Morning Scotland* operates as the equivalent of Radio 4's *Today Programme*. In ways analogous to the Scottish broadsheet press, Radio Scotland's morning news programme has a major agenda-setting role. Significantly, it attracts four times more Scottish listeners than its London-based counterpart.

BBC Television Scotland provides a distinct news service and some current affairs programmes, as well as other programmes such as drama, music, comedy and sport. However, by contrast with the comprehensive Scottish national radio service, it takes the bulk of its programming from the two BBC UK networks, opting-out with specific programmes for Scottish viewers. It also supplies network programming, notably drama and comedy. While the Scottish ITV stations retain a regional remit, the 'national regional' BBC Scotland takes the whole country as its territory in news and current affairs coverage, such as the early evening flagship news programme, *Reporting Scotland*, and the current affairs programme, *Frontline Scotland*.

The BBC's role under a devolved Parliament was summed up thus by the Controller, Scotland, John McCormick, in November 1997: 'Our aim is to ensure that we provide an unrivalled journalistic service that matches the new pattern of governance of the UK'.[21] The centrality of journalism both accords with the corporation's public service mission and the BBC's global strategy of developing its presence as a news and information provider. Certainly, there is no intention of departing from the BBC's unitary structure. McCormick has stated that according to audience research the corporation is valued as an organisation by the Scottish public, and that there is no demand to break it up. However, since BBC Scotland describes itself as the cornerstone of the broadcasting industry in Scotland, it has also recognised that its activities will be properly scrutinised by the Scottish parliament. But this is not seen as replacing the existing form of accountability through the Governors to the Secretary of State for Culture, Media and Sport. Scottish Television similarly sees itself as continuing to be regulated through the ITC, whose chairman, Sir Robin Biggam, has dismissed the prospect of separate Scottish broadcasting regulation, while conceding that national sensibilities will have to be addressed.[22]

While Scottish Television initiated the debate on the journalism most suited to Scotland's new political landscape, it is BBC Scotland that has followed up the issue in detail by creating working groups to assess parliamentary coverage, newsgathering, the pattern of news output, and weekly current affairs. Gus Macdonald remarked to me that SMG intended to await the outcome of the BBC's review in spring 1998 before deciding on its own course of action. According to McCormick, the reviews will open a period of consultation with the audience.

Although on the more fundamental question of regulation, the BBC, like SMG, has followed the White Paper and the Scotland Bill, which have reserved broadcasting powers to Westminster, this has been challenged by the SNP, which tabled an amendment to the Scotland Bill. The party considers that in order to protect the national culture, both public sector and commercial broadcasting should be under the legislative control of Edinburgh. This argument will probably gain impetus. However, the SNP has not indicated how it will take account of the long-standing British tradition of arms-length broadcasting regulation, which differs considerably from direct parliamentary control.

The SNP is presently making the running on Scottish media policy issues. Aside from the Liberal-Democrats' general expressions of concern about media concentration and the maintenance of ITV's federalism, both Labour and the Conservatives seem content with the status quo. But this complacency is likely to be shaken up as the UK regulatory regime is generally rethought due to policy initiatives taken by the European Commission. Scottish, British and EU media policy dynamics will therefore intersect in the run-up to the creation of the new parliament. If substantial changes occur in the broadcasting field at Westminster before the Edinburgh legislature first convenes, this will probably cause political problems.

Currently, in line with the government's view embodied in the Scotland Bill, BBC Scotland, Scottish Television, and Channel 4 have so far rejected any radical change either to broadcasting finance or control. However, pressure for a more or less radical shift of powers to Edinburgh is bound to continue. Debate is likely to be fuelled by the activities of the Campaign for Broadcasting in Scotland, which has argued for the devolution of structures. The Campaign's chairman, Nigel Smith, has proposed that BBC Scotland controls both the Scottish license fee and the scheduling of network services in Scotland and that Channel 4 develops a distinct Scottish service on the lines of the Welsh S4C.[23] The SNP's George Kerevan, fronting the media pressure group, Voice for Scotland, has argued for the Scottish parliament to have a say in the forthcoming renewal of the ITV franchises. The consumer lobby, Voice of the Listener and Viewer, has latterly provided a platform for discussion of broadcasting and devolution. Such interventions are a foretaste of what is to come.

From political culture to politicised market-place

While it is too early to judge how Scotland's much-mooted 'new politics' will develop, rhetorically, at least, important gestures have been made. The watchword from Donald Dewar, the Secretary of State for Scotland, and Henry McLeish, the devolution Minister, has been 'accessibility'.

Dewar has said of political reporting that 'We are not likely to wish to recreate the lobby system'.[24] It remains to be seen precisely what arrangements will be worked out with the new Scottish Parliamentary Press Association. McLeish, for his part, has considered how cable and digital technology might be used to increase public access. Scottish Office ministers have also talked of opening up the parliament to pressure groups and the public.

The potential for Scotland to develop a distinct information regime under its own legal system was rather dramatically illustrated at the beginning of 1998. English media were unable to name the British Home Secretary, Jack Straw, when his son had been charged with a drugs offence. However, the legal constraints did not apply north of the Border. *The Scotsman*, *Daily Record* and *Scottish Daily Mail* decided to break the wall of silence (already breached on the Internet and in foreign newspapers), precipitating UK-wide media coverage. Legal differences apart, what would enable Scotland to set a different course would be a political consensus on greater freedom of information in Edinburgh, made easier by the absence from the parliament's remit of such security-obsessed areas as foreign affairs, defence and finance.

The use of the additional member system in parliamentary elections— modifying Westminster's first-past-the-post tradition—and the apparent determination of the 'Yes-Yes' parties both to ensure a gender balance in Edinburgh, as well as to employ a more consensual style in parliamentary committees, could all contribute to giving Scottish political culture a quite distinctive style and flavour. In such programmatic strands, the continuing influence of the Constitutional Convention is still perceptible. The Referendum brought the SNP into the parliament-building fold through collaboration in the umbrella group, Scotland Forward.[25] The post-Referendum inquest on the Scottish Conservative Party under Lord Strathclyde has ensured that it, too, will use the new arena to relaunch itself. A four-party parliamentary dynamic, with each party vying to devise the most authentically popular Scottish policies, will look strikingly different from Westminster, and may well lead to new political alignments.

It is already clear that the Scottish parliament will be a focus not just for the news media, but that it will reorientate the whole gamut of activities from public relations and lobbying to marketing and advertising to telecommunications. Devolution will enhance the country's international recognition and, internally, a strengthening sense of Scottishness will mean that proximity to consumers is essential for companies eager to exploit national tastes on behalf of their clients.

Consequently, communications companies have been keen to establish themselves in Scotland. Of the mainstream media, Channel 4 has made an adaptive gesture towards devolution by establishing a new office in Glasgow, with Stuart Cosgrove as Head of Programmes (Nations and Regions). There is a widespread expectation in the creative community that the increased relevance of national identity will be reflected in the broad range of films, radio and television output.

The political market-place is also developing, with political and public affairs companies keen to exploit the new opportunities. Moves are afoot to set up an association of professional lobbyists and civic groups, and bearing recent Westminster experience in mind, to try and establish a 'sleaze-free' rule-book. There is also increased interest in setting up think-tanks to influence the policy process. Not only has there been a growth of activity in advertising and marketing firms, but also in the reprofiling of telecommunications. For instance, BT has declared its interest in the restoration of trust in the political process, and underlined the role of IT in promoting electoral involvement through training and education and remote working of MSPs. Already evident, therefore, in anticipation of the Edinburgh legislature's opening, is an intricate and intimate relationship between a reshaped political culture and a wider political market-place. This new institutional nexus will become a key part of Scotland's civil society and a major dimension of a redrawn national communicative space.

The New Labour obsession with 'rebranding' Britain has found its modest northern counterpart in the focused marketing of Scotland. Currently, research is being undertaken by the Scottish Enterprise-funded body, Scotland the Brand, into 'Scottishness' and its exploitability in advertising and the packing of Scottish goods. The underlying aim, endorsed by the Scottish Office, is to bring together the marketing of trade, tourism and culture. Although, confirmed devolutionist that he is, Donald Dewar situated Scotland's branding in the context of UK government policy, he also made it clear that it was in response to Scottish national promotional needs. Scotland the Brand's new country of origin device, unveiled in November 1997, is the word 'Scotland', in signature style, in which Saltire blue gives way to tartan. The logo is intended to be used across the range of products and services—food, drink, textiles, financial and medical services, engineering, the universities—and while it has yet to win widespread support, by December 1997 it had been already adopted by 150 companies.

The choice of tartan as one of the official manifestations of Scottishness—which has aroused negative reactions from those concerned about a modern image of Scotland—is discrepant with the Blair Government's self-styled modernism. During the Commonwealth Heads of Government Meeting, held in Edinburgh in October 1997, New Labour decided to ban thistles, tartans and bagpipes as outmoded, provoking the SNP leader, Alex Salmond, to condemn the obliteration of Scottish symbolism. The present focus on political regeneration, it is plain, is closely and complexly connected with both cultural awareness and the business dimension, and fertile ground for contention.

Concluding remarks

The boundaries of political communication in Britain are undergoing profound—and largely unremarked—change. I have argued that there are two main causes that underlie this process. First, the European Union is redefining both British domestic politics and media agendas. And second, the devolution of powers to Scotland is producing a new *national* parliamentary centre. As a result of the latter, the fault-lines running through British statehood will become much more apparent as 'north of the Border' comes to signify wide-ranging democratic autonomy for the Scots.

Even before it is in place, the very prospect of Scotland's parliament is promoting the creation of an increasingly distinctive political culture, one that defines itself as *not*-Westminster. It is an open question whether ultimately the new constitutional settlement will push the wider British polity in the direction of federalism, or instead lead to Scottish separation. Whatever the eventual outcome, we are already facing a change of historic significance that will unleash a new political dynamic and reshape national identities both in Scotland and in the UK as a whole.

Within multi-national states such as the UK, it is plain that nationhood and statehood may pull in divergent directions, creating new fields of force. In the process of 'stateless nation-building' that is entering a decisive phase in Scotland today the reconfiguration of politics has been intimately related to media and communication.[26] For instance, consistent media coverage in Scotland certainly played a major role in preparing the ground for the Referendum. The strong support for devolution showed that there was an informed public, precisely because of the airing given to the lengthy debate (both pro and con) amongst the political classes, key interest groups, and the intelligentsia.[27] By contrast, the radical implications of devolution are not so well understood south of the Border, where media attention has been somewhat sporadic and rather superficial. There is at present a communication deficit which may have important consequences for relations between the parliaments at Westminster and at Holyrood and also for how the different parts of the UK react to major political change. Arguably, therefore, 'cross-border' communication via the news media will have an increasingly crucial role to play in the reporting and interpretation of devolution within the United Kingdom.

Following the Referendum, there were indicative tensions in the political dealings between Edinburgh and Westminster. There was a serious squabble over the control of inward investment between the Scottish Office and the Department of Trade and Industry. A key debate also opened up over the 'Barnett formula' that determines per capita expenditure in the different parts of the UK: the present favouring of Scotland led to serious questioning of current arrangements by English MPs, and was a foretaste of the much more fundamental discussion to come concerning the country's financial settlement under devolution. These issues, and others, attracted levels of media attention in Scotland far greater than those in England, a disequilibrium in public communication that gives cause for concern.

From a quite different angle, we might note how, following publication of *Scotland's Parliament*, and moves prior to the enactment of the Scotland Act in 1998, the imminent prospect of devolution rapidly led to an emergent debate about Scotland's future media regime. To date, this has touched on regulation, the concentration of ownership, regionalism, the organisation of political reporting, and broadcasting economics.

However, so far as both broadcasting and the press are concerned, the parameters of policy change are located not at Westminster alone, but also increasingly in Brussels. Ultimately, therefore, the options available to Scotland's media will be influenced by a context in which global economic competition and technologically-driven change will be decisive counters, as will supranational processes of political and economic integration. The present drive towards technological 'convergence' in the fields of broadcasting, telephony and information technology will be determined by the outcome of the debate over the European Commission's November 1997 Green Paper on regulation.[28] The Brussels initiative has raised questions about whether current regulatory systems are blocking the growth of an information society. It has also brought to the fore concern about the place of cultural and social goals in a new European media order. Another policy issue, that of the concentration of media ownership, is also set to come back into the frame. This is the latest stage of the European Commission's long-running, and so far inconclusive, attempt to grapple with how to devise rules able to secure pluralism in a wide variety of European media markets.

Both of these grand themes—'convergence' and 'concentration and pluralism'—with their interweaving of media, communications and cultural policies, have been on the political agenda for much of the 1990s and will continue to be so in the new millennium. The terms of the debate—national cultural defence v techno-economic determinism; information pluralism v media concentration—will be played out at three articulating levels: the EU, the UK, and the Scottish. Consequently, how Scotland's transforming politico-communicative space is elaborated will depend not only on London, but also significantly on Brussels.

Acknowledgements

I am grateful to Jean Seaton for her careful questioning and insightful editing, and above all, for her enthusiasm for this contribution. My thanks, too, to Peter Meech for saving me from some infelicities. The chapter has also benefited from participants' comments made at *The Political Quarterly*'s conference on 'Politics and the Media in Britain: the Next Five Years', held at St Catherine's College, Oxford, in September 1997, and at the ESRC 'Media Economics and Media Culture' Programme's workshop on 'Political Communication and Democracy', held at Stirling University in November 1997.

Biographical note

Philip Schlesinger is Professor of Film and Media Studies and Director of the Stirling Media Research Institute at Stirling University. He has written widely on the media and politics. His books include *Putting 'Reality' Together*, *Televising 'Terrorism'* and *Media, State and Nation*.

Notes

1 Karl Deutsch, *Nationalism and Social Communication: An Inquiry into the Foundations of Nationalism*, Cambridge, The MIT Press, 2nd edn., 1966; Ernest Gellner, *Nations and Nationalism*, Oxford, Basil Blackwell, 1983; Benedict Anderson, *Imagined Communities: Reflections on the Origin and Spread of Nationalism*, London, Verso Editions, 1983; Michael Billig, *Banal Nationalism*, London, SAGE Publications, 1995.
2 Jürgen Habermas, *The Structural Transformation of the Public Sphere: An Inquiry into a Category of Bourgeois Society*, Cambridge, Polity Press, 1989; John Keane, *The Media and Democracy*, Cambridge, Polity Press, 1991.
3 The present chapter has been researched with the support of the Economic and Social Research Council's 'Media Culture and Media Economics' Programme. Issues raised here have been fruitfully discussed with my colleagues Brian McNair, David Miller, William Dinan and Deirdre Kevin in the 'Political Communication and Democracy' research project team, but responsibility for this analysis is mine alone. The support of the Norwegian Research Council's ARENA Programme is also gratefully acknowledged.
4 Jürgen Habermas, 'Citizenship and National Identity', pp. 20–35 in Bart van Steenbergen, ed., *The Condition of Citizenship*, London, SAGE Publications, 1994.
5 Philip Schlesinger, 'From Cultural Defence to Political Culture: Media, Politics and Collective Identity in the European Union', *Media, Culture and Society*, 1997, pp. 369–91.
6 At present, this doctrine officially concerns member states' relations to the Union. However, it is plainly open to inventive appropriation at the sub-state level, and will affect how the 'Europe of the Regions' shapes up.
7 Anthony Barnett, *This Time: Our Constitutional Revolution*, London, Vintage, 1997.
8 *Scotland's Parliament*, Cm 3658, Edinburgh, The Stationery Office, 1997.
9 Kenyon Wright, *The People Say Yes: The Making of Scotland's Parliament*, Argyll Publishing, Glendaruel, 1997; James G. Kellas, 'The Constitutional Options for Scotland', *Parliamentary Affairs*, 1990, pp. 426–34.
10 *Scotland Bill*, House of Commons, Session 1997–98, Internet Publications, 18 December 1997.
11 David McCrone, 'Unmasking Britannia: the Rise and Fall of British National Identity', *Nations and Nationalism*, 1997, pp. 579–96.
12 Michael Keating, 'What's Wrong with Asymmetrical Government?', paper presented to the ECPR Standing Group on Regionalism, conference on 'Devolution', Newcastle-upon-Tyne, February 1997; David McCrone, *Understanding Scotland: The Sociology of a Stateless Nation*, London, Routledge, 1992; Lindsay Paterson, *The Autonomy of Modern Scotland*, Edinburgh, Edinburgh University Press, 1994.

13 Peter Meech and Richard Kilborn, 'Media and Identity in a Stateless Nation: the Case of Scotland', *Media, Culture and Society*, 1993, pp. 245–59.

14 John McInnes, 'The Broadcast Media in Scotland', *Scottish Affairs*, 1993, pp. 84–98.

15 These figures, and those in the rest of this section, are based on the National Readership Survey's figures for Daily and Sunday Newspapers in Scotland for July 1996–June 1997.

16 *Guardian*, 29 July 1996.

17 Figures and quotations from his speech to the Voice of the Listener and Viewer Conference on 'Broadcasting in Scotland Post Devolution', Stirling, 29 November 1997.

18 Maurice Smith, *Paper Lions: The Scottish Press and National Identity*, Edinburgh, Polygon, 1994.

19 Andrew Neil, *Full Disclosure*, London, Pan Books, 1997. Quotation from pp. xvii–xviii.

20 *Broadcast*, 29 September 1997.

21 John McCormick, 'The BBC and the Changing Broadcasting Environment', University of Strathclyde, Town and Gown Lecture, 4 November 1997.

22 *The Scotsman*, 3 January 1998.

23 Nigel Smith 'Broadcasting and a Scottish Parliament', *Scottish Affairs*, 1997, pp. 29–41.

24 Quoted from his reply to questions at the CREST conference on 'Understanding Constitutional Change', Edinburgh, 21 November 1997.

25 The post-Referendum consensus was somewhat shaken when, in January 1998, Donald Dewar announced the choice of Holyrood as the site for the Scottish parliament. This was controversial because of the anti-nationalist political motivations attributed to the decision in some quarters. Both the Liberal Democrats and the SNP had favoured Calton Hill, home of the Royal High School, which was to have been the Assembly building in 1979, and had been the symbolic focus of political campaigning since then.

26 Michael Keating, 'Stateless Nation-building: Quebec, Catalonia and Scotland in the Changing State System', *Nations and Nationalism*, 1997, pp. 689–717.

27 Contrast the Scottish vote with that for the Welsh Referendum, where the 'Yes' vote prevailed by the narrowest of margins. Moreover, in January 1998, the accuracy of the Welsh count was being questioned.

28 European Commission, *Green Paper on the Convergence of the Telecommunications, Media and Information Technology Sectors, and the Implications for Regulation: Towards an Information Society Approach*, Com (97) 623, Brussels, 3 December 1997.

Dumbing Down or Reaching Out: Is it Tabloidisation wot done it?

STEVEN BARNETT

EVERY now and then a word or phrase appears which, quite suddenly and unexpectedly, seems to capture a mood. In October 1994, the *Guardian* included 'dumbing down' in its glossary of the nineties, a phrase imported from across the Atlantic where it had been used consistently over the last 5–10 years to describe a pervasive sense of declining cultural, educational and political standards.

In fact, the *Guardian* was ahead of its time. In the five years from the beginning of 1990 to the end of 1994, the entire UK broadsheet press could muster only 11 references to 'dumbing down' between them. The tally rises to 27 in 1995 and 23 in 1996, not enough to suggest that a defining statement about the state of 1990s Britain had arrived. But in 1997, it took off: the British broadsheet press saw over 400 references to 'dumbing down'.

Its origins are in concerns around standards in schools rather than the media, first surfacing in the letters pages of the *Independent on Sunday* during correspondence on the role and significance of the humble apostrophe. One contributor could barely contain his fury at the illiteracy of another: '[He] exhibits not only ignorance of the purpose of punctuation in general and the apostrophe in particular, but also parts of speech . . . His letter seems to advocate a further "dumbing down" to meet declining literacy in a rapidly declining education system.' Further references were prompted by American concern about the lowering of educational expectations in their schools. One American professor, concerned about the dumbing down of school curricula, concluded that schoolbooks were written 'at the level at which a farmer talks to his cows'.

Thus, the context for a discussion about 'tabloidisation' of the media is a more widespread anxiety about our educational, political and cultural environment. This is important, because concerns about declining standards in the media go back at least to the launch of the *Daily Mail* in 1896 and the ferocious debate which surrounded the introduction of commercial television in 1955. Furthermore, the almost relentless pessimism in which this debate is being couched leaves no room for a less negative interpretation of the 'tabloidisation' theme: that we are seeing a more accessible, less elitist approach to communication. Are we really witnessing the kind of wholesale evacuation from more challenging cultural and educational ideals that recent debates about the scale of 'dumbing down' would have us believe?

This chapter does not pretend to answer that question. Rather, I want to disentangle some of the questions raised by the 'tabloidisation' thesis in order

© The Political Quarterly Publishing Co Ltd 1998
Published by Blackwell Publishers, 108 Cowley Road, Oxford OX4 1JF, UK and 350 Main Street, Malden, MA 02148, USA

to inject a little cautious scepticism. First, what does it mean? Because it is a term frequently deployed about many different aspects of media output, it is likely to conceal rather different meanings and manifestations. There is always the temptation—as with crime statistics, respect for teachers, the richness of political discourse or the quality of the England cricket team—to believe in a mythical golden age. It is important to break the concept of tabloidisation into more tangible (and if possible empirically verifiable) terms. Secondly, what are the possible causes? Are there features of late 20th century Britain that might explain either the 'fact' of tabloidisation (in its different guises), or the outpouring of concern over its perception? This is not just an academic debate about semantics or the role of a healthy, pluralistic media. There are policy choices which flow from a proper understanding of the 'problem' and its causes, but these cannot be sensibly considered if the media are subjected to ill-defined and unsubstantiated charges of descending into the gutter.

The Problem

There are at least three separate strands to the tabloidisation argument which need to be disaggregated and then challenged. First, is the assumption that the 'bad' is progressively chasing out the 'good', i.e. that we are witnessing a process of displacement in which more emphasis is placed on entertainment, showbusiness, scandal and prurience at the expense of more serious, challenging material like current affairs, policy issues, the arts, or foreign affairs. We are talking here about the selection of material rather than the way in which subjects are covered or prioritised. Thus, broadsheet newspapers are supposedly devoting more coverage to areas that traditionally were the stamping ground of tabloids: the traumas of various Royal Family relationships, the sexual antics of British film stars and politicians, the highs and lows of pop music personalities, the details of particularly lurid murders or sex crimes. While the lure of the famous and the bizarre has always proved irresistible to the popular press, the broadsheet press has, the argument goes, resolutely resisted such vulgarity. The same is said of the broadcasting industry in general: that airtime—in particular peak television hours—are being given over to entertainment shows and soap operas, that the emphasis again is on the big personalities, show business and big sporting events. If America is Britain's role model, a recent forum held at Columbia University's School of Journalism suggests there is much to fear: a 42 per cent reduction in foreign news coverage on the three major networks between 1988 and 1996, and a sad recognition by the senior executives present that 'time and money dictates we must bypass some stories' because that's what the viewers want.

There is, however, no concrete evidence of such displacement in the UK. This is important, because we need to consider the real possibility that the massive expansion of airtime in broadcasting and pagination in the local and national press is obscuring the continued availability of 'serious' material. In the UK, in the ten years from 1984–94, almost every national newspaper increased its number of pages by at least 50 per cent. Some, like the *Guardian* and *The Times*, more than doubled in size, while the *Mail on Sunday* and *Sunday Express* more than tripled.[1] It is only relatively recently that TV channels have become 24 hour operations, and the addition of daytime and breakfast schedules as well as the surge of new satellite channels have produced a spectacular increase in television airtime. All these pages and channels need to be filled, but not necessarily at the expense of material that was previously available.

We therefore need to ask whether, as appears to be true in America, we are really seeing fewer pages devoted to foreign affairs in the press, fewer international stories in the news bulletins and less emphasis on international issues in analysis programmes or opinion pages. Are foreign correspondents finding it more difficult to get their material aired or published? Or is that perception being created by the sheer weight of entertainment material which might seem overwhelming, while in fact there has been no change in the *absolute* level of more serious material available? It is certainly possible to devise a research study which could test this thesis, as has already been done in the field of children's programmes. In that instance the 'tabloidisation' thesis was confirmed when the authors discovered that cartoon and entertainment formats had doubled on children's television in BBC1 and ITV *at the expense of* other approaches such as story telling, preschool and factual programmes.[2]

The second argument is that, whether or not the *volume* of serious or challenging material has declined, its nature is being debased through various packaging and presentational strategies to make it more populist. In a stinging attack on what he calls the 'news thieves' of network television, the veteran American foreign correspondent Mort Rosenblum has documented some depressing examples of foreign news coverage in the US: how Roone Arledge, president of ABC news, told his news anchors to describe Sarajevo as 'site of the 1984 Olympics' to help the poor souls whose knowledge of geography East of America stopped at the Statue of Liberty; or how another network's definition of foreign news included stories from Chicago, Northern Maine and Outer Space.[3] In Britain, Bob Franklin quotes a senior press journalist's claim that 'the constant injunction from editors these days . . . is to keep every story BLT—to keep it bright, light and trite' while the BBC's foreign editor John Simpson has said that when news organisations' reports start going below two minutes, it is an 'infallible sign' of going downmarket. On a more abstract level, ITN has been accused more than once of using progressively more patronising language in its bulletins for ITV.

Length and language, then, are supposedly ingredients of the shift towards tabloidisation, but again there is a different interpretation: that journalism—and particularly tabloid journalism—has a long and honourable history of making difficult concepts or stories 'come alive' for people who lack either the ability or inclination to read long-winded articles on complex subjects. Political advertising, for example, is condemned for reducing complex social and economic issues to 30 second chunks of emotive language and sensationalist images which are devoid of meaning and obscure any real policy thinking. But if the purpose of such ads, like news bulletins aimed at large audiences, is to convey the substance of an issue in a manner which is comprehensible and attractive to audiences, there is surely an argument that this is a potentially democratising and enfranchising shift rather than a debasement. Most Americans understood the essence of Bill Clinton's campaigning message in 1992 that 'trickle-down economics' had not worked. Most Britains did not have a clue what Labour's (then) shadow chancellor meant by 'endogenous growth theory' in 1996.

The lighter touch, and its use in leavening an otherwise serious approach, has not been exclusive to commercial television or the tabloid press. One of the BBC's most successful news programmes was the daily magazine programme *Nationwide* which interspersed serious items on government policy with others like the now infamous skateboarding duck. Any theory of tabloidisation must find a way of addressing a journalistic tradition which has always tried to emphasise the importance of introducing stories through personal histories, real-life dramas or humour. In the 19th century rhyme which Matthew Engel used to illustrate the philosophy of popular journalism over the last hundred years: 'Tickle the public, make 'em grin, The more you tickle, the more you'll win'.[4] It does not necessarily follow that tickling must always entail some kind of degradation of journalistic endeavour.

There are two more, quite subtle, variations to this argument that the nature or quality of serious material is being degraded. The first has been prompted by a string of 'sleaze' allegations aimed at people in authority. Can a distinction be made between, on the one hand, legitimate enquiries about improper private behaviour that might interfere with a person's ability to conduct their public life competently, and on the other a growing obsession with the private lives of prominent people in order to satisfy the mass audience's apparently voracious appetite for voyeurism? Scandal has always made good copy, especially sexual scandal. But there is mounting concern that what used to be an appetite tempered by some respect for the pressures of high office is turning into ruthless victimisation as tabloid journalists seek to expose every dalliance, cupboard skeleton or human weakness of those in the public eye.

Thus Hugo Young, surveying the acreage of newsprint about Lorena Bobbitt and the severed penis, Michael Jackson and his alleged abuse of children, Gillian Taylforth's motorway antics and the bizarre circumstances of MP Stephen Milligan's death, argued that the media were creating 'a theatre of cruelty' which was more than just sexual gossip. It was as if pleasure was increasingly being derived from the infliction of pain or embarrassment on public figures, that we were becoming addicted to stories which ruin other people's lives. 'What is developing is a search-and-destroy journalism which probes for weakness and then moves in to hunt and harrass'. The process is even more insidious because it poses as serious, investigative journalism which demands time and money. While journalistic resources are then deployed in 'digging the dirt' on minister X or soap opera star Y, the more serious enterprises of uncovering corruption or miscarriages of justice are ignored. The result is an impoverished public culture where authority appears to be mired in sexual corruption, while other improprieties go unexamined and unpunished.

The second strand also concerns an impoverishment of public life through the apparent diminution of a critical or sceptical approach to journalism. This charge was levelled in particular at reporting of the Gulf War, which was widely perceived as being driven by the telegenic and spectacular pictures of computerised missiles hitting their targets with accompanying commentaries informed almost entirely by military sources. War reporting has always had to strike a delicate balance between not endangering security while trying to maintain a critical distance from official sources, but most journalistic self-reflection after the event was concerned about the extent of unwitting collusion. More recently, the professionalisation of political party communication strategies has entailed a number of carrot and stick tactics designed to 'tame' political journalism: the awarding of favours (interviews with key figures or exclusive stories) to those offering the most helpful coverage, opprobrium and exclusion for those who persist in ignoring the 'party line' and adopting a more sceptical approach to party briefings. The result is, potentially, a servile press who are less willing to challenge governments or their policies.

The third argument is that, even if the quantity of serious coverage has stayed constant and its nature remains uncorrupted, serious stories and programmes are being given progressively less prominence. In an effort to ensure that front pages and peak-time programmes do not alienate potential readers or viewers, they are being given over to more entertaining or more lurid or more 'human interest' stories. This is an important distinction, because it suggests that serious, analytical or more difficult stories are still being covered, but are being relegated to the margins of TV and radio schedules or the inside pages of newspapers and magazines. Availability is therefore not a problem for the discerning seeker after serious information; they simply have to look more carefully at the small print on page seven or stay up later at night to get it.

Particular targets here are the front pages of broadsheet newspapers, the running orders of the main evening news bulletins and the peak time schedules of the mass audience broadcasters. The charge is that, where 10 or even 5 years ago, quality newspapers would give front page priority to important political debates, foreign stories or new policy initiatives, today's are much more likely to be dominated by allegations of sleaze, the latest round of marriage break-ups in the Royal Family, or a major crime or tragedy story, all belonging firmly to the tabloid tradition. Meanwhile those more serious programmes which have managed to avoid complete abolition, like Granada's *World in Action* or London Weekend's *South Bank Show*, are being shifted to the margins of the ITV schedule.

The Definition

All of these arguments about the 'fact' of tabloidisation are premised on certain predefined notions of 'good' and 'bad', which themselves are predicated on assumptions about the potential benefits that the media can bring to society. Whether certain kinds of stories are being displaced or demoted could be tested by a longitudinal study of newspapers and news bulletins, but there are hidden definitional risks in an apparently simple process of counting minutes or column inches. A good example is television current affairs. My own research for the ITV Association, which looked at trends in terrestrial TV schedules from 1985 to 1995, suggested that there had been almost no reduction in current affairs programmes during the most deregulatory period in British television history. What it did not examine were any changes in the kinds of issues which current affairs programmes were tackling, and where journalistic resources were being directed. British television—and in particular British commercial television—had nurtured an impressive reputation for important journalistic exposures: miscarriages of justice, incompetent health and safety practices, the humbuggery and hypocrisy which are practised in most companies, governments and organisations. All have been—or had been—legitimate targets for exhaustive investigations by ITV companies even at the risk (as in the infamous case of Thames TV's *Death on the Rock*) of provoking a savage government backlash.

The role of journalism to ask embarrassing questions and challenge those in authority is one of its most fundamental tasks in a democracy. If, indeed, these kind of investigations are being driven out of the television schedules by a different interpretation of current affairs—with greater emphasis on issues like the rise in house prices or a crisis in the monarchy—this would be fairly conclusive proof of the tabloidisation thesis. But even within a stricter definition of campaigning journalism, we are left with a problem of definition. How would any study deal with stories about the Royal Family? Given the traditionally tabloid material that the royals have been providing over the last ten years, a current affairs programme could easily be classified as a perfect example of ratings-driven tabloid television at its most excessive. But what if the programme consisted of a balanced and well-made film on the history and constitutional position of the monarchy followed by an informed discussion amongst those seeking its reform, abolition or continuation? What if it contained a great deal of carefully researched information about, say, the cost to tax-payers of maintaining the Royal List versus the revenue derived from tourism and the benefits for charities with royal patrons? It is certainly arguable that, whatever the nefarious aims of certain republican proprietors, the British tabloid press provided a public service in exposing some of the greed, hypocrisy and financial waste that seemed to be associated with at least some elements within the Royal Family. The approach may have been soap opera, but the effect of demystifying a British institution for which tax-payers foot the bill might equally be defended—and in some quarters vehemently was—as a classic example of great investigative journalism.

A graphic illustration of how journalists themselves grapple with these definitional problems—and how the concept of 'tabloid' can be interpreted both positively and negatively—comes from television news. On 25 November 1993, a school minibus crashed on the M40 motorway killing at least ten teenagers and their teacher. This happened to be the same day as the Queen's Speech outlining the government's plans for the coming session of Parliament, and the aftermath of an IRA bomb which exploded in Warrington. ITN led its main evening bulletin on the crash. The BBC led with the Queen's Speech followed by the Warrington bomb. The M40 crash came third.

Thanks to the *Independent on Sunday* three days later, we have access to a fascinating internal debate which followed on the BBC's computer system and which reveals some of the thinking—and disagreements—which surround editorial decisions.[5] There was one group of journalists who found the decision 'bizarre' and dismissed the argument that, because the decision was shared by all the next day's broadsheet press, anything else would have been a 'tabloid approach':

Tabloids are read by more than 10 times as many people as broadsheets, and we're supposed to be a public-service broadcaster, i.e. accessible to a large part of the population. It's not taking a 'tabloid approach', for God's sake, it's just about acknowledging what ordinary people . . . want to know about.

Another disagreed with the decision on different grounds:

It seems to me the best yardstick for judging news importance is to ask yourself what contemporary historians will see as the most important event which occurred on this day. The death of a dozen people in a road accident must rate higher than the Queen's Speech.

But the most passionate language came from those who felt that the news values were so self-evident 'when 10 children die' that any other decision was simply incomprehensible: 'if you'd made that decision in any radio or newspaper newsroom I've ever worked in, you'd have faced the sack'. By contrast, one of those supporting the decision also argued on the basis of news values but this time broadsheet values: 'Any day or night editor of a broadsheet who ran the crash as front-page lead ahead of the Queen's Speech would have been hauled up before his superior faster than you could say "tabloid".' Another supporter saw the debate in terms of the longer term significance of each story:

Some of us just happen to think that when the Government sets out what it's going to do—i.e. the myriad number of ways it's going to screw us over—in the next year, it's important enough to lead a news bulletin with.

This exchange goes to the heart of the argument, not just about prioritising stories, but trying to find some workable non-derogatory definition of 'tabloid'. Should we approach the argument on the basis that stories of human tragedy, which are likely to attract massive public interest simply because of the sympathy they generate for ordinary people suddenly becoming the victims of extraordinary events, nevertheless represent a somehow less elevating, less citizen-enhancing role? Perhaps the journalistic instinct of pursuing the unfolding story simply because it is a story is, in fact, itself a 'tabloid' instinct. If so, if this debate is to have any meaning, we have to define an approach for journalistic endeavour which is predicated on a particular role for journalism and the media in society: presumably one based around concepts of citizenship, democracy, knowledge enhancement and personal enrichment rather than simply the conveyance of information to audiences about things that might interest them. This, however, needs to be made explicit and may well be challenged on grounds of elitism or paternalism. Nevertheless, even if we rightly regard the fact of tabloidisation with some scepticism, it is possible to identify a number of root causes which could be having the effect of degrading public discourse.

The Causes

Conventionally, any shift downmarket tends to be ascribed to competition for audiences. There is, goes the argument, a cycle of inevitable decline as more newspapers on smaller margins chase a declining number of readers and a vast array of television channels compete, not just with other programmes, but electronic games and interactive computers. The result is spiralling standards as editors and programme makers increasingly seek out the formats with the greatest appeal to the largest number of people and abandon anything which might, by virtue of being more difficult or challenging, risk alienating potential consumers.

As an argument in isolation, competition is not convincing. There has been vigorous competition for readers in all sectors of the newspaper market since before the First World War, and in broadcasting since 1955. If anything, the pattern in newspapers has been the closing down or merging of new titles, so that the broadsheet market—with the addition of the *Independent*—is little different from 50 years ago. True, a plethora of satellite TV channels have come on stream in the last ten years, but these are almost all funded by subscription and have not proved particularly threatening to the long-standing audiences of terrestrial channels. The start of Channel Five in 1997 is the first real threat to mainstream television audiences, but arguments about the downward drift of television long predate its arrival. If the argument about tabloidisation is that it is a progressive trend, there have to be other causes as well as—or allied to—more competition to explain the changes.

There have been at least four such changes. The first, which has been apparent throughout European broadcasting in the 1990s, is the gradual relaxation of regulatory regimes which used to lay down strict criteria for the balance of programming on commercial channels. In the UK this process had a fundamental impact on ITV, particularly its enviable record for hard-hitting investigative reporting in its two current affairs strands. In 1993, a new 'lighter touch' Independent Television Commission replaced the old Independent Broadcasting Authority, but most attention focused on the sudden creation of a competitive market-place in commercial television: ITV companies were forced to bid large sums of money in a competitive auction for their licences and then compete with a newly separated Channel 4 for advertising revenue. At the time, it was these financial and competitive pressures which led us all to issue dire warnings about the downmarket plunge of a cash-strapped ITV while regarding the ITC as a recycled if slightly less bureaucratic IBA. Ironically, as it transpires, ITV has had very few money problems. What it does with the money, and the absence (if it can be proved) of high quality investigative journalism has more to do with the shift in regulatory culture.

The IBA was designed to foster a culture of excellence, to instil in ITV companies aspirations in programme-making which they might not freely adopt. It was, in the modern political jargon, an enabling framework, which set standards and helped to create an environment in which the best producers in the industry could flourish. The IBA spelt out for ITV companies what was required and expected of them.

The ITC is a different animal. It has no role in fostering quality, just a set of paper promises and a remit to monitor output retrospectively. It is a body which sets minimum, rather than aspirational, standards in an industry where yardsticks of measurement are notoriously hard. The model for the ITC is the new breed of consumer watchdog, another OFGAS or OFWAT, designed to prevent abuses rather than promote excellence. There are no brownie points to be had for exposing government corruption or security services incompetence in some foreign land, especially if it involves losing potential viewers. Even before the new regime was implemented, Carlton's then director of programmes Paul Jackson insisted that current affairs programmes could only keep their peak-time place through consistently high ratings. He told the *Daily Telegraph* in 1992: 'If *World in Action* were in 1993 to uncover three more serious miscarriages of justice while delivering an audience of three, four or five million, I would cut it. It isn't part of the ITV system to get people out of prison'. We can hardly be surprised if the consequence is a less hard-hitting style of journalism on ITV (and now Channel 5).

Meanwhile Channel 4, which continues to be highly regulated by Act of Parliament and a new set of even tighter interpretive guidelines, continues to produce some excellent examples of difficult journalism: Martin Gregory's Torture Trail in the *Dispatches* strand was a recent example, as was the scheduling of a whole week of peak-time pre-Christmas viewing devoted to a series of programmes about Bosnia. That a wholly commercial channel can produce such programmes and make them so accessible is a tribute not to Channel 4's revenue, but to the regulatory framework that sustains it.

The second change is bound up with the first. As competition intensifies throughout the media industry and broadcasting regulation is relaxed, decisions become more consumerist. The public become 'consumers' and what they want, how programmes, newspapers or articles can be better packaged to draw more of them in, becomes the guiding principle. This has often been true in the newspaper industry, but there has emerged over the last twenty years a new, more scientific consumerism built around the burgeoning business of market research, database marketing and highly sophisticated audience research information capable of almost infinite computer analyses. 'Targeting' and 'branding' have become part of the vogue media vocabulary, now applied as much to channels and even individual programmes as to newspapers. Just as British Rail's passengers and the National Health's patients have been transmuted into customers, so senior editorial personnel will now hold forth on the place of their 'product' in the 'new marketplace'.

The result is a focus group mentality which has seeped from business into the media and, of course, into politics. If focus groups tell us that one Brit carries the news value weight of ten Americans, 100 Germans or 1000 Algerians, we steer our news bulletins and current affairs programmes in that direction and adopt the same attitude as the *Sun* columnist Richard Littlejohn: 'Does anyone really give a monkey's about what happens in Rwanda? If the Mbongo tribe wants to wipe out the Mbingo tribe then as far as I am concerned that is entirely a matter for them.' If focus groups (and computer analysis of ratings) tell us that our coverage of the Olympic Games alienates too many women, we adopt NBC's approach to feminising its 1996 coverage by offering, in the words of NBC's head of sport 'not sports but stories about sports'. He told the *New Yorker* that 'with apologies to Jane Austen, our version of the Olympics is about sense and sensibility'. And if focus groups tell us that the news is too middle aged, middle class and too confrontational—as the BBC discovered in February 1997—then you talk about targeting the 'c1/c2 25–44 age group' with more user-friendly politics.

At its most extreme, the audience-centred approach requires editorial decisions which cannot challenge the viewers' or readers' conventional wisdoms, in case it is somehow alienating. According to a *Guardian* story in 1992, the BBC tried to sell to the Discovery Channel its six-part series *Living Islam*, a version of Professor Akbar Ahmed's study of Islamic life and thought. Discovery, an American education channel, rejected it with the following argument from its representatives: 'For us, Islam means terrorism, fundamentalism and the mistreatment of women. If you can't major on that, we don't want to know.' These kinds of arguments, founded on a belief that the assumed prejudices and limited knowledge of audiences cannot be disturbed, are hardly conducive to an uplifting or informational role for the media.

The third change arises partly out of the first two: the increasing power of advertisers to determine the nature of editorial content. The gradual withdrawal by broadcasting regulators who used to be interposed between advertisers and programme makers has allowed advertisers greater freedom in their dealings with producers and channels. Sponsorship, which just ten years ago was stringently regulated, is now commonplace, with advertisers prepared to spend considerable sums to have their names associated with programmes which are commensurate with their 'brand values'. That, in turn, means that programmes which might prove to be offensive or upsetting to certain audience groups—however well made or artistic they might be—become commercially less attractive. When Channel 4 showed *The Last Temptation of Christ*, it provoked 6,000 complaints to the channel itself and 1,400 to the Independent Television Commission. The directors of 33 major businesses which bought airtime during the film received letters asking why. Big advertisers like Tesco, Mars and Peugeot were reputedly annoyed that their commercials had been aired during such a controversial film.

Talking about the newspaper industry over ten years ago, James Curran argued that the expansion of editorial space had been geared to advertising potential, representing 'an efficient means of selling selected subgroups within a mass audience, packaged in a suitable editorial environment. Their advertising orientation has encouraged the specialist journalists working on these pages to develop a dependent and generally uncritical relationship with advertisers'.[6] This influence was, he argued, even more marked in the magazine press. Since then, newspapers have expanded still further with even more emphasis on consumer and leisure pursuits, while the new satellite thematic channels offer exactly the same specialist environment for advertisers. With regulatory insulation removed from broadcasting, it would be surprising if advertisers did not impart their generally safe and comfortable editorial values to areas of commercial TV, just as they have in the press.

There is another strand to this extension of commercial, or corporate, values into commercial media. Beyond traditional advertising and marketing techniques looms the burgeoning industry of public relations. The influence of PR is in many ways more insidious because it is, by definition, unseen. While advertising and sponsorship are overt, paid for, attempts to convey a message from a readily recognisable source, PRs work behind the scenes to persuade the information providers—journalists—of the merits of their clients' case and to ensure their clients' receive 'appropriate' publicity. The photo opportunities and spin doctoring of modern political campaigning are the most notorious manifestations, but are less dangerous precisely because of their notoriety. More pertinent are the free trips abroad for transport correspondents, the personal briefings over sumptuous lunches for business writers, the exclusion from the big fashion events of critical fashion correspondents; and such headline-making activities as abseiling in the House of Lords (members of a lesbian activist group) or transatlantic voyages in hot air balloons (a well-known entrepreneur). Attention grabbing techniques and image presentation are not new, nor in themselves undesirable. What has changed is the professionalisation and employment of, probably, millions of people devoted to the cause of creating or changing images rather than reality. Their primary targets are media outlets and their gatekeepers—the journalists.

That these gatekeepers are almost certainly becoming more vulnerable to the blandishments of a burgeoning PR industry is partly due to the fourth change: the speed with which journalists have to work and the volume they have to produce to service proliferating media outlets. Technological change has transformed the professional practices of journalists in different ways. Where previous deadlines for daily print journalists may have been early evening, it is now common practice for a breaking story to be updated into the early hours of the morning. In broadcasting, the sheer volume of pro- grammes, channels and stations devoted to news means journalists are expected not just to provide material, but to keep a story moving. Steve Richards, now the *New Statesman*'s political editor, compared coverage of John Major's perennial 'leadership crisis' in 1993–5 with that of Harold Wilson's 25 years earlier when Wilson was at his most vulnerable. He concluded that 'The leadership crisis which engulfs John Major every few months is nurtured and sustained by the massive expansion in broadcasting outlets. The political interview . . . is now so commonplace that one feeds off another, constantly renewing a sense of political crisis and providing fresh copy for newspaper journalists'.[7] It means that every word, inflection or hesitation by politicians is scrutinised for evidence of splits or disagreements which can then be turned into bigger stories. The informational or democratic value of such 'stories' are practically nil.

In foreign reporting, mobile satellite technology guarantees not just that no part of the world is inaccessible to TV cameras, but that reporting is instantaneous. The result can often be dramatic, live pictures which provide little hard news and obscure the absence of any informed or critical reflection, as in the Gulf War. The problem is not just the speed of transmission, or even the pressure to be 'first with the story' (which has always been an honourable aspiration amongst professional journalists). It is what appears to be an increasingly careless and compromised approach to journalistic accuracy. The sex scandal which has enveloped President Clinton has followed a frenzied, speculative and uninformed approach—in the absence of virtually any corroborated evidence—which stands in stark contrast to the 'two reliable sources' rule which governed the Watergate exposés of the Washington Post 25 years ago. A combination of more competing news outlets and new technology may be conspiring to produce a more irresponsible, compromised approach to publication before checking facts.

Two further factors are at work which are not new but may be exacerbating a drift towards tabloidisation over the last few years. The first is ownership, and the particular news values of proprietors. While competition to increase readers and viewers may in itself drive media outlets to seek more populist formats, there is some evidence that the particular values of those who own the media—and through them the senior editorial staff—will permeate the newspapers and stations they own.

The clearest documented evidence is the influence of Rupert Murdoch. While attention is usually focused on how he determines the political line of his media interests, there is more interesting (and damaging) evidence of his own approach to journalism and how he inculcates those values in his editorial teams. His biographer William Shawcross, generally thought to have produced a favourable portrait, has described his aversion to serious investigative or challenging journalism. He is contemptuous of those who seek to expose corruption or wrong-doing in high places and, says Shawcross, 'believed that Watergate-type investigations were not the purpose of journalism'. Murdoch's papers could not attract first class journalists because 'the ethos of News [Corporation] discouraged independent investigation or troublesome journalism'.[8] How this philosophy seeps into his papers is well illustrated by an anecdote from ex-Times journalist Michael Leapman:

In 1977, when Elvis Presley died, I was working for *The Times* in America and suggested that I might go to Memphis to cover this seminal event and the reaction to it. 'Sorry', I was told. 'Not a *Times* story'. Four years later, when Bob Marley died, not only was I sent to Jamaica for his funeral but when I arrived I found another *Times* writer there, assigned by the arts section. Rupert Murdoch had acquired the paper two months earlier.[9]

Every proprietor will take his media interests in a direction that is profitable and maximises readership or viewership. But the degree of titillation, triviality, sensationalism or vulgarity which such an approach to journalism might entail will still depend on the tolerance levels of individual proprietors.

The role of government patronage should not be underestimated. This, again, is hardly a new phenomenon in broadcasting and should—according to committed free marketeers—be on the wane as the market place takes over from state regulation. We should distinguish, however, between the relaxation of regulatory frameworks—which are not under direct government control—and actual or threatened statutory intervention. With media conglomerates becoming increasingly strident in their demands for greater laxity in, for example, cross-media ownership legislation or the freedom to move News at Ten, the attraction of making life difficult for the very same government starts to fade. It means that the scope for government sponsored favours to media entrepreneurs is probably greater than it has ever been. A more competitive media system probably offers less, rather than more, protection against government interference. The communications revolution, in the words of John Pilger writing after the Gulf War, 'has produced not an information society but a media society in which . . . the vocabulary of state and vested-interest manipulation is increasingly elevated above that of free journalism'.

Conclusions

When Kelvin MacKenzie, at the height of his reputation as editor of the *Sun*, gave evidence to the Calcutt Committee on Privacy, he made a pointed contribution: 'Tabloid journalism cannot be condemned simply because it is brash or noisy or declamatory. It must only be called to order if it is false, irresponsible or reports untruths.'[10] Therein lies the problem for anyone seeking to argue or demonstrate that the quality of our public culture is being progressively eroded. There may be plenty of potential reasons why standards of journalism might have declined, but we have to be very careful to find a way of defining what this process of corrosion actually represents which is not simply a condemnation of the popular.

While attempts at quantification—for example of levels of foreign news coverage, or the number of peak-time current affairs programmes devoted to policy issues—may allow for some tentative conclusions, they will always be predicated on some subjective assessment of what constitutes a healthy journalistic culture in a thriving democracy. On that basis, if we are trying to establish the evidence for tabloidisation, a more productive approach may be to complement any 'objective' study with an analysis of intent: what are the prime purposes of the programme makers, journalists, editors and owners who are responsible for creating the material we watch or read? If these come down solely to the maximisation of readers and viewers for selling on at the highest price to advertisers—with little or no thought for how content might have to be distorted or debased in order to increase its attraction—the resulting material is unlikely to have much value beyond pure escapist entertainment. The chat shows which now dominate much American daytime television and feature such themes as teenage prostitutes and women who marry rapists, are an example of a genre aimed solely at provoking the greatest display of outrage—preferably involving on-screen violence—in order to generate press coverage and increase ratings. The philosophy for such shows are illustrated by the notice pasted up on the production office of the Jerry Springer Show: 'No subject too indecent, no individual too pathetic for THIS show.' While talk shows can be both popular and address issues and dilemmas of everyday importance, programmes like Springer's make no pretence that they are contributing to public debate. They are simply cash cows.

If we pursue the notion of intent, then the corollary of such naked, unthinking populism might best be characterised as 'integrity'. As in the debate between BBC journalists on news bulletin running orders, this does not disqualify arguments about populism or accessibility. It does, however, force the editorial decision-makers to ask themselves questions about their purpose. Writing about the problems afflicting foreign reporters faced with faster technology and increasing competition at home, Martin Bell wrote recently:

It does no harm for all journalists . . . to ask ourselves a simple question: What do we believe in? If it is only making money, then we are clearly in the wrong business because money can deflect, if not corrupt, us. But if we have standards and values and principles, then we should stand by them because they are what we believe in and what sustain us. There is actually a word for it. The word is *integrity*.[11]

Bell believes that American networks, driven by the exigencies of profit maximisation, have abandoned foreign reporting with the result that 'The American people are significantly worse informed today than they were twenty years ago'. Recent research has confirmed that, compared to six other advanced industrial democracies, Americans are indeed the least knowledgeable about foreign affairs, and that this is at least in part directly attributable to the impoverished nature of foreign news reporting on American television.[12] The reason, following Bell's argument, is that journalists and editors of those programmes no longer see any value in what they do beyond generating the largest possible number of recorded viewers to deliver to advertisers.

How do we sustain the integrity that is the life-blood of enlightened (and enlightening) journalism? Partly, it requires reinforcement as part of a professional ethos of journalism, learnt through training and bolstered through professional codes of practice. But even when aspiring to the most noble professional values, journalists cannot be impervious to the institutional pressures of news editors, channel controllers, editors-in-chief and ultimately owners. Whether it be fear of government retribution (the BBC), fear of jeopardising a proprietor's business interests (News Corporation), fear of offending an advertiser or simply the pursuit of profit, even the Martin Bells of this world are subjected to compromising influences from above and require a sympathetic framework which can support their highest aspirations. Ultimately, that must come down to a regulatory system which recognises that in the cultural industries the unfettered pursuit of profit is unlikely to produce the opportunities for knowledge and understanding that an informed, effective, participatory democracy requires. It is an old argument which was lost in the 1980s and needs to be revisited now, with some creative thinking about what regulatory or statutory initiatives might be feasible. Perhaps ultimately it scarcely matters whether we can define 'tabloidisation' or whether there is incontrovertible evidence for its existence. What is important is to prevent—or at least constrain—the conditions under which an erosion of public culture is likely to happen or continue further.

Biographical Note

Steven Barnett is senior lecturer at the Centre for Communication and Information Studies, University of Westminster and co-author of 'The Battle for the BBC'.

Notes

1 Bob Franklin, *Newszak and News Media*, London, Arnold, 1997, p. 90.
2 Jay Blumler, *A Review of Children's Television 1982–92*, London, Broadcasting Standards Council, 1992.
3 Mort Rosemblum, *Who Stole the News?*, New York, John Wiley and Sons, 1993.
4 Matthew Engel, *Tickle the Public: one hundred years of the popular press*, London, Victor Gollancz, 1996.
5 'How bad is the Nine o'clock News?', *Independent on Sunday*, 28 November 1993, p. 4.
6 James Curran, 'The impact of advertising on the British mass media' in Richard Collins et al., eds., *Media, Culture and Society, a critical reader*, London, Sage, 1986.
7 Steve Richards, 'Soundbite Politics', Reuter Foundation Paper 14, Green College, Oxford, 1995.
8 William Shawcross, *Murdoch*, London, Chatto and Windus, 1992.
9 'Gossip or news? Who can tell?' in *Independent on Sunday*, 8 September 1996, p. 19.
10 Quoted in Raymond Snoddy, *The Good, the Bad and the Unacceptable*, London, Faber and Faber, 1992.
11 Martin Bell, 'The Truth Is Our Currency' in *Harvard International Journal of Press/ Politics* 3(1): 102–109, 1998.
12 Michael Dimock and Samuel Popkin, 'Political Knowledge in Comparative Perspective' in S. Iyengar and R. Reeves, eds., *Do the Media Govern?*, Thousand Oaks, Sage, 1997.

Monarchy and the Message

BEN PIMLOTT

ARE the mass media killing off the British Monarchy, or has the Monarchy—in its desperate fight to retain a hold on the public imagination—brought most of its problems on itself, by mismanaging its media relations? The modern history of Palace-press dealings can be used to support both theories. Thus, if editors are to be held responsible for switching from craven adulation to prurient derision in order to boost sales, the Palace can equally be blamed for naivety or complacency, and for helping to create a bubble of unreal expectations that was bound to lead to disillusion sooner or later.

There is also a third, less judgmental, interpretation of the Monarchy's image problem: namely, that it has been caused, not by unwise policies—or even by the misadventures of individual family members—but by changes in the technology and economics of mass communications over which neither courtiers nor editors have ultimate control. By this interpretation, there could scarcely be a more salutary illustration of the way a revolution in the medium revolutionises the message, than in the treatment of the royals in recent times. The tale is important in itself, politically and constitutionally; it also has a direct bearing on the development of national, political and general-interest news.

There is no beginning to the story. The Monarchy, of course, pre-dates the media, but it has always been concerned about public opinion. Since the institution lost the bulk of its political power, it has depended for its survival on the success of its public relations; and the Court has appreciated the value, as well as danger, of public curiosity. There would be little point, after all, in a national symbol, if the nation ignored it, or a constitutional Royal Family, if its members were not seen as private individuals as well as public figures. That has been one side of the equation. The other has been the desire of people born or married into the *ménage* to preserve a part of their lives, behaviour, and emotions, from public scrutiny.

Dogs

What is legitimately private? The issue—for a Monarchy that used to eat, ablute, consummate its marriages, seduce its mistresses, even give birth to its progeny more or less in public view—has never been simple. The Court became reticent on such matters in the eighteenth, and especially, the nineteenth centuries. Yet it always maintained an element of double standards: there was no objection to the publication of private details, provided they were the right ones. What it sought to do was to release appropriate

Published by Blackwell Publishers, 108 Cowley Road, Oxford OX4 1JF, UK and 350 Main Street, Malden, MA 02148, USA

information, while filtering out the rest. A code became established during Victoria's reign, based on an unspoken Establishment understanding with a small group of British-and-Empire based newspaper owners, and on a belief among editors that the public would be offended by the publication of material the Royal Family wished to withhold. Thus lurid rumours of a kind that gain automatic headlines today—about the *amours* of the Prince of Wales, for instance, or the alleged link between the Duke of Clarence and a male brothel in Cleveland Street specialising in telegraph boys—were passed over in decorous silence. Such an arrangement continued with remarkably little disturbance after Victoria's death. The First World, dislocating in many other ways, seemed to strengthen it. During the reign of George V it came to be forgotten that Queen Victoria and her eldest son had often been the cause of ribaldry ('an elderly widow and an unemployed youth', Walter Bagehot called them). Criticism of the public behaviour of the Monarch, let alone of his behaviour in private, vanished from the public presses. Hence Buckingham Palace had little difficulty in choosing the glimpses of royalty it wished to be known, and hiding the rest.

Providing such glimpses was taken seriously, as a practical necessity as well as a duty: if there was little criticism of George V, that was partly because there was no repetition of the withdrawal of his grandmother, following the death of Prince Albert. The nation was in particular need of a dependable Sovereign, and that was how he, and his family, were seen and described. Queen Mary was presented as a paragon of motherly wisdom, her children as loyal and patriotic. Thus, the marriage of the King's second son, the Duke of York, to Lady Elizabeth Bowes-Lyon, in 1923, was choreographed with the Empire's newspapers in mind.

When the Yorks had children—third and fourth in line to the Throne—the picture papers made their faces as familiar to the public as those of William and Harry are today: and not just their faces, but also well-honed versions of their characters, from an early age. A variety of judicious anecdotes encapsulated their supposed natures, and were included in sanitised biographies that sold like hot cakes before the girls had reached puberty. Such works had a serious public relations intent: *Our Princesses and their Dogs* (1936), made much of the children as typically English pet-lovers; while a book by Captain Eric Acland, chronicler by appointment, called *Princess Elizabeth* (1937), provided the supposedly intimate secrets of a typically English upbringing. ('Once Lisbet had been naughty, for even princesses can be naughty', wrote the author, in the characteristic idiom of this kind of writing, 'and her mother, to punish her, refused to tell the usual bedtime story'.[1])

The girls were also quite deliberately used for wider political purposes. One major media event of the Princesses' childhood was the construction, by Welsh craftsmen out of Welsh materials, of a miniature Welsh cottage, with miniaturised furniture, pots and pans. Months of well-orchestrated publicity preceded the hand-over of this toy to Elizabeth, as a birthday present 'from the people of Wales'. The donation was followed by extended

© The Political Quarterly Publishing Co. Ltd. 1998

photo-sessions, showing the Princess and her sister mothering child sub-
stitutes (corgis) in the doorway, or playing at being Welsh housewives. The
pictures were not merely cute. They were intended to underline the Royal
Family's concern for a Principality currently ravaged by depression and
unemployment.

J. M. Barrie images of royalty were balanced by an alternative picture of
royalty as reassuringly elderly and wise. Thus the celebration of George V's
Jubilee in 1935 linked a tradition-minded old man with national claims to
continuing world power and military strength. Parades, street parties and
firework displays took place across the Empire, and were widely reported in
the picture papers, alongside photos of the whole Royal Family. The wireless
(George V had recently established himself, through annual Christmas broadcasts, as the first radio king), air travel, and ever-improving land and sea
communications, helped the orchestration of the world-wide celebration,
bringing the Monarchy to an apex of popularity.

However, such an exceptional whipping-up of excitement around an
institution that depended on myth, made the institution vulnerable if the
myth was undermined. When George V died in January 1936, mourning was
mixed with eager anticipation: the Empire's papers were filled with admiring
profiles of his eldest son, a man idolised, in the words of one commentator, 'as
few men outside the Orient ever have been'.[2] The café-society style and
matinée good looks of Edward VIII, which had already made him the star of
the newsreels, encouraged hopeful predictions of a modern and modernising
Monarch. People remembered the new King's insistence, confronted with the
poverty caused by closed mines, that 'something must be done'; they did not
know about his petulance and unreliability, or his relationship with the
divorced American, Mrs Simpson, because these had not been reported in
the press.

Abdication

In retrospect, world-wide interest in the British Monarchy, combined with
improved access to foreign media, meant that the story of Edward's
inappropriate romance could not have been kept out of the British papers
forever. At the time, royal advisers fervently hoped that it might. For a while,
ferocious gossip took the place of the printed word. 'Those who most
strenuously maintained a decorous loyalty in public', the republican editor
of the New Statesman, Kingsley Martin, recalled, 'were the most avaricious of
scandal about the Monarchy in private'.[3] The King's own refusal to take
elementary precautions helped to ensure that the dam would burst. When it
did, there was a turning-point: the assumption that British royalty should
have an automatic immunity from damaging stories abruptly ended. Arguably, the recent history of press coverage of royalty, and of royalty's moral
dilemmas and nervous resistance to scrutiny, has been an extended sequel.

'To engineer the abdication of one king and the enthronement of another in six days', wrote Beatrice Webb in her diary at the time, 'without a ripple of mutual abuse within the Royal Family or between it and the Government, or between the Government and the Opposition, or between the governing classes and the workers, was a splendid achievement, accepted by the Dominions and watched by the entire world of foreign states with amazed admiration.'[4] But if it was a splendid achievement, much of the credit—so editors, at any rate, believed—was due to the press, which had brought a matter of importance to the attention of the public, and forced the Prime Minister to bow to the power of proprietors he had once compared to trollops.

Superficially, there was little change. For the time being, the press remained as respectful in its treatment of royalty as ever. This was partly because the disgraced King's successor provided little reason to be anything else. Luckily for the Palace and Establishment, the new Monarch turned out to be what one contemporary observer called 'a Symbol King'.[5] George VI was a man of slow intellect and nervous temperament, but with a profound sense of duty and a keen awareness that the Monarchy's continued existence now depended on its willingness to do what was expected of it. Edward VIII had teased the press. His brother, by contrast, meekly acknowledged his dependence on its goodwill. International crisis helped to ensure that he got it. Over the next fifteen years—a period dominated by, war, fear of war and the aftermath of war—the new King was able to provide a point of reassurance, not by what he did, but by his passive acceptance of what the emergency required of him and his family.

'[W]e all went on to the Balcony where *millions* of people were waiting below', wrote the eleven-year-old Princess Elizabeth in her diary, following her parents' Coronation. 'After that we all went to be photographed in front of those awful lights.'[6] Before George VI's accession, it had been possible for the Yorks, as they then were, to lead a comparatively normal upper-class life. Now 'those awful lights' became an unavoidable part of their world. The young princess was left in no doubt about what to expect: the significance of mass communications was soon drummed into her as part of a hastily-concocted preparation for future responsibilities. In special history tutorials at Eton, the Vice-Provost, Henry Marten, taught her that the two most important recent developments affecting the Monarchy were the 1932 Statute of Westminster, which established the modern Commonwealth, and the advent of broadcasting, which enabled the Royal Family to sustain its new Commonwealth links by talking personally to the Dominions on the air.

During the Second World War, the Ministry of Information reinforced Marten's teaching by publicising the private world of the Royal Family as the ideal to which every home-loving serviceman or woman, and every freedom-loving civilian, might aspire. Images of royal familial happiness became part of the universal iconography: in her Amsterdam hideout, Anne Frank pinned cut-outs of the little princesses to the wall. Had Edward VIII stayed King, he might have been used differently. As it was, the King, Queen and their two daughters, portrayed around a roaring fire, often with a radio set to hand, were distilled and exported as the essence of home-front Britishness.

With the deepening crisis, the propaganda value of royalty increased. Queen Wallis might, perhaps, have been used for an American tour: Princess Elizabeth, aged 14, was used for a celebrated North American broadcast. In October 1940, the BBC employed her to read a speech ostensibly directed at British evacuees, but actually aimed at US Congressmen and editors. The broadcast, which assured thousands of children separated from the parents, that 'in the end all will be well,' produced headlines in every American newspaper and was hailed as a triumph. Encouraged, the British Government made increasing use of the names and pretty faces of the two royal children in its morale-boosting publications and make-and-mend economy campaigns, at home and throughout the Empire. As well as supporting the war effort, such a policy reinforced a world-wide sense of the British Royal Family as the perfect domestic hearth. So much so, that fantasy and reality seemed to merge: visitors to Buckingham Palace, overjoyed to be in the presence of a family about which they had heard such heart-warming reports, were readily enchanted, while the Windsors responded by performing appropriately. Thus, the officially-disseminated impression of a happy family that had never been happier or closer than in the grimmest days of a terrible war, or more prepared to share its warmth with those in need of it, may not have been far from the truth.

Spring-blossom

In such conditions, making the private public was a tactic that worked: not all that was private, but an important part of it. Covered up were George VI's speech impediment, shyness, and explosive outbursts of bad temper (courtiers called them his 'gnashes'). Visible were the activities the family shared together: gardening, riding, playing with pets, gymkhanas in Windsor Great Park. One notable private activity, of which the public were made aware, consisted of a series of amateur Christmas pantomimes written by a local schoolmaster and staged by the princesses and local children at Windsor. These began early in the war as cheerfully ramshackle affairs for family and staff, but were soon turned into part of the royal display. Private became public with a vengeance: weeks before the 1943 pantomime, advance press publicity produced a thousand letters from the public, many containing blank cheques, asking for tickets.

The Royal Family emerged from the war with enhanced prestige: the King and Queen were admired for their stoicism, their daughters for their spring-blossom beauty and for symbolising the generation for whom the war had been fought. Edward VII was seldom mentioned in the press, not so much rejected—his role as a colonial Governor was presented as a patriotic service—as quietly forgotten. Once again, radio played a key part. During the royal South African tour in the summer of 1947, Princess Elizabeth's 21st birthday broadcast from Cape Town, in which she made a 'solemn act of dedication with the whole Empire listening', might have been a Henry Marten schoolroom essay. As the official censorship ceased, an element of mischievous enquiry about the Heiress's romantic intentions entered the popular papers. But there was no departure from habitual press respect, despite the election of a Labour Government, committed to increasing equality and reducing hereditary privilege. Indeed, so far from attacking the Monarchy, the press seemed to appreciate it all the more, and the public turned up in increased numbers at royal ceremonials. When Princess Elizabeth became engaged to Lieutenant Philip Mountbatten in 1947, the administration responded to the public mood by deciding that a people's princess needed a people's wedding and hence the Heiress's marriage—a 'splash of colour', Churchill called it, against the drab backcloth of austerity—became a media event comparable only to the Jubilee.

Intense press coverage focused on material objects: the Gifts, the Cake and—above all—the Dress. Spurred on by newspaper accounts and pictures, a permanent queue the length of the Mall formed outside St James's Palace, where the wedding dress was put on public show. On the day itself, radio was once more the dominant medium, listened to by the entire nation, and much of the rest of the world. Mass Observation reported clerks huddling round the office set to catch every word of the ceremony, and there were accounts of ships hoving to mid-Atlantic so that all the crew could get a good reception. 'Television's magic crystal'—as The Times called it—was still in its infancy, though a TV camera over the Palace forecourt, and another outside the Abbey, covered key moments. More important was film, both in Britain and abroad. Immediately after the event, newsreels of the procession were flown across the Atlantic by special carrier, for distribution to cinemas throughout the United States.

Thus, in the late 1940s, the first signs of a new prosperity, and the emergence of a handsome young couple, helped fast-developing media to turn the world's premier royal family into icons of a new era. For the moment, traditions of reticence were strictly maintained: when Princess Elizabeth accompanied her husband to Malta, where he was stationed as a naval officer, the press left her alone, and she was able to live something approaching a normal service life, driving her own car round the island or dining at a local hotel without being bothered by reporters. The respite, however, was short-lived: as before the war, hugely overheated popularity caused a dangerous momentum. Reticence might still be the rule at home: abroad, different standards applied. In 1949, the American Ladies Home Journal serialised extracts from The Little Princesses, a memoir by the former Marion Crawford ('Crawfie'), who had been governess, mentor and companion to the royal children for a decade and a half. As in 1936, US publication was swiftly followed by publication in the United Kingdom. Though Crawfie's book contained little which today would be regarded as objectionable, it marked a watershed: 'doing a Crawfie', hitherto virtually unknown, became a form of betrayal that it was impossible to prevent.

To a large extent, the problem over royal privacy was a direct product of the royal insistence on preserving it. Like the thrill to be gained from lifting the skirt of a piano leg, Crawfie's book caused a *frisson* because of the tightness with which royal privacy had been guarded, and a reluctance to see anything but the most sugary version of it to appear in print. The instrument of this policy was the King's press secretary, Commander Richard Colville, known by journalists as 'the Abominable No Man', and later inherited by the King's eldest daughter. The Crawfie episode seemed to have a traumatic effect on him: instead of encouraging greater flexibility, it produced even more censorious prudery. Colville, 'ashen-faced and like the wicked uncle in a pantomime', as Cecil Beaton described him in 1953, '. . . who deals so sternly with all of us who are in any way connected with the Press',[7] remained in the royal service until 1968. His legacy—a belief among newspaper editors that any item of below-stairs gossip was likely to be of interest, because of the frantic concern of the Palace to suppress it—continues to have its baleful effect. Yet an essential protection remained in place: the ultimate arbiters of what went into newspapers, the readers, still preferred to get positive, dignified and supportive news about royalty than the reverse.

Hemlock

When George VI died in February 1952, and his mother, Queen Mary, died a few months later, the press went into suitable mourning. The black drapery of coffins and catafalques was replicated in black borders round the front pages of newspapers and magazines, but not for long: in the spring of 1953, sombre shades were replaced by celebratory and patriotic red-white-and-blue. The Coronation of Elizabeth II—colourful awakening of affluence, final parade of Empire—heightened the association of Monarchy and Royalty with youth, modernity and hope.

It also helped to define the media. In 1947, television had been a curiosity, a minor adjunct to film and radio. In 1953, it became the medium which everybody—rich and poor—sought to watch. At first, the new Queen was reluctant to allow the cameras into the Abbey, and both Cabinet and Church backed her up: it was felt that crowning-over-the-coffee-cups would detract from the dignity of the event. The people demanded a people's Coronation. Faced with an unexpected torrent of letters to the editor and parliamentary questions, the Queen was persuaded to change her mind. The result was a media revolution that transformed the industry, and permanently altered the way in which the public would perceive royalty and royal events.

The Coronation was the first event seen by the majority of the population. In Britain an estimated 27 million people watched the Coronation live for at least half the day, and a European link-up extended coverage to much of France, West Germany and Holland. It became the national occasion that everybody remembered, partly because of the excitement of seeing the new medium. Television licence-holders doubled from 1 million to 3 million in anticipation, and many people who rented sets for the occasion decided to retain them. The expectation that royal events would be televised became automatic. At the same time, royal iconography altered. Hitherto, apart from flickering cinema newsreels, the imagery had been largely static. Now it became animated, and the Royal Family-in-motion became one of the most familiar symbols of public life.

Television also heightened the tendency, already apparent in the reigns of the Georges, to see the Monarch as close to divine. Never before or since has a King or Queen combined so little actual power, with so little opposition, and so great an aura. 'For the first few years of her reign', as the historian Sir Charles Petrie put a few years later, 'she was the subject of adulation unparalleled since the days of Louis XIV.'[8] It was as if any questioning of the role or style of the pinnacle of the British Constitution combined blasphemy, subversion and bad taste: except that there wasn't any questioning, outside the extreme-left press. Sycophancy filled every crevice of the media, encouraged by an overwhelming popular mood: editors and programme makers discovered that the more gushing and mawkish the copy, the bigger the audience they could obtain. Yet there was one chink: if the Monarch herself was placed on a pedestal, her relatives did not have the same immunity, at a time when a public craving for royal human interest was pushing the media with greater intensity than ever before.

The breaking of the story of Princess Margaret's interest in Peter Townsend, a divorced equerry, followed a now-established pattern. The American press broke it first, whereupon the British press felt justified in following suit. At the wedding of Lord Mountbatten's daughter Patricia, early in 1947, a simple gesture, caught on film—Prince Philip helping Princess Elizabeth with her coat—stoked the rumours of an impending engagement. Six years later, a sharp-eyed reporter noticed Princess Margaret brushing some fluff off Townsend's lapel in the ante-room to the Abbey on the day of the Coronation, and the result was a New York headline next day which led Fleet Street to pass on the message that the Queen's sister 'is in love with a divorced man and that she wishes to marry him'.

The critical word was 'divorced': hemlock to Royalty. It took the public back seventeen years, and excused, on grounds of public interest, editorial decisions to be prurient.

The Townsend relationship was media-led from the moment it became public, until it was called off: every development in the story was chronicled in detail. Coverage of the Wallis-Edward affair had been quickly over, ended by a swift prime ministerial decision. By contrast, the Margaret-Townsend sage spread over two and a half years. The press presented the issue as political, constitutional and above all religious. What sold papers, however, was the star quality of the Queen's sister. Margaret's combination of royalty,

98

beauty, style, flirtation with the cameras (what Cecil Beaton called a 'sex twinkle of understanding in her regard')[9] and a troubled soul, were irresistible.

The relationship evoked a characteristically double-barrelled response: lip-smacking in the popular press, moralising in the qualities. New techniques were pioneered—including the doorstepping of royals under pressure because of their private lives. At the time of Margaret's twenty-fifth birthday in August 1955, when the Princess became legally free to decide her own marriage partner, three hundred pressmen converged on Balmoral, where she was staying. 'Come on Margaret!' demanded the *Daily Mirror*, 'Please make up your mind!' But it was *The Times* that sealed her fate. In October, an unctuous leading article by Sir William Haley, the editor, declared that a union with Townsend would be one 'which vast numbers of her sister's people, all sincerely anxious for her lifelong happiness, cannot in conscience regard as a marriage'. After reading these words, the Princess—'mindful of the teachings of the Church'—formally surrendered. It was an important defeat, reinforcing the media triumph of 1936: each time, important royal decisions were hastened if not forced by the press. On both occasions, precedents were set and, thereafter, slavishly followed.

In its relationship with royalty in the second half of the present century, the media have followed a firm principle: if you get away with something once, raise the stakes and try again. The Margaret-Townsend episode showed how fragile the code of decorum protecting royalty really was. Indeed, so far from precluding any mention of royal scandal, the post-Coronation conditions of royalty-worship had turned fringe-royal private lives into dynamite. Other members of the family also became targets: the Margaret affair had barely died down, when rumours of an alleged infidelity by the Duke of Edinburgh swept around the globe. Yet again the American press led, with a report about a supposed liaison with an unnamed woman in the flat of a well-known photographer, and a 'rift' in the Duke's marriage. After the *Baltimore Sun* had splashed, several (though not all) British papers ran with it.

Schoolgirl

The Monarch herself was left alone: young, impassive, impeccable, solemn beyond her years, she was considered untouchable. However, a couple of attempts were made to bring a sense of perspective. In the summer of 1957, the young editor of the *National and English Review*, Lord Altrincham (now John Grigg, the distinguished historian), published an article which put into words what many were privately thinking.

The personality conveyed by the utterances put in the mouth of the Sovereign, wrote Altrincham, was 'that of a priggish schoolgirl, captain of the hockey team, a prefect, and a recent candidate for Confirmation'.[10] A delicious outrage dominated the media for weeks. When an angry member of the public struck Altrincham in the street in front of newsreel cameras, the incident received major headlines. ('Smack!' exulted the *Mirror*, in a banner headline. 'Lord A. gets his faced slapped.') The pot was given a stir during a royal tour of the United States, when Malcolm Muggeridge, a veteran *enfant terrible* of British journalism, wrote in the New York *Saturday Evening Post* that 'Duchesses find the Queen dowdy, frumpish and banal',[11] and blamed the royal set-up for enduring aspects of social class.

An important aspect of the Altrincham-Muggeridge episode was the attitude of the BBC. The Corporation was proud of its special relationship with the Palace, and conscious of the role its coverage of royal events had played in the expansion of television, as well as in fending off the recently-established independent channel. At stake were exclusive rights to royal events, and in particular the highly-prized Christmas Day Broadcast, which the Queen had just agreed to have televised. A bid by commercial television in 1957 had just been repelled.

Confronted by Altrincham and Muggeridge, the BBC were deeply embarrassed. There was a dilemma: would they lose more of their audience by ducking a controversy, or—if they embraced it—by losing royal favour? A debate raged within the Corporation, with deep implications for the future of royal broadcasting. At first, the two offending writers were banned from the airwaves. After what was felt to be a decent interval, they were allowed back, but on the strict understanding that they avoided mentioning the Monarchy. Thereafter, producers were bound by an edict from the Corporation's Director of Current Affairs, Harman Grisewood, that it was 'not proper or fair to broadcast a discussion, pro and con, about the conduct of the reigning Monarch'.[12] The fear that the Queen's advisers would freeze out the BBC, or—worse—transfer its patronage to the opposition, remained as a powerful inhibition. 'Any clash with the Palace', as an internal BBC memo warned in 1958, 'is likely to jeopardise our future requests'.[13] For the next thirty-eight years—until the Diana crisis—versions of this principle continued to underlie the Corporation's treatment of royal issues.

Yet, paradoxically, there were also countervailing forces at the BBC that pushed the other way. While some broadcasters anxiously defended their special privileges, others were engaged in a guerrilla war against the attitudes on which the privileges depended. The avalanche of changing values—the so-called permissive revolution—that occurred in the 1960s owed much to broadcasting, and especially to the BBC's famous satirical show *That Was The Week That Was*, which altered the rules of engagement between media and the Establishment, and made everybody seem fair game. Meanwhile, the election of a Labour Government in 1964 caused other ramparts to crumble.

One target was the Lord Chamberlain system of licensing plays, which precluded, on grounds of public taste, acting that was deemed too overtly sexual, and the portrayal on the stage of any twentieth century Sovereign. The bizarre coupling of sexual and royalty censorship was unfortunate for the Monarchy. In the 1960s, the literary and theatre world were considerably more incensed by the first restriction than by the second. However, the obvious absurdity of the royalty ban encouraged the use of royalty-satire to express the general defiance. Those who wished to make their point by causing offence also took royalty-acting onto the streets, and got the result they hoped for. As late as 1967, a plan to represent the Queen in a political demonstration in Trafalgar Square brought the threat of police action.

Fly-on-the-wall

In the following year, the Lord Chamberlain system, already in tatters, was finally abolished. The theatre was now free to act out royal scenes, and act our sex. Were there to be any limits? The position was hazy, but the tabloid press—faced with an increasingly relaxed public attitude, and no clear laws— nibbled at the edge of surviving taboos. Growing ease of access to foreign broadcasts and publications made the taboos harder to defend. In the same year that theatre censorship ended, the *Daily Express* published a family snap of the Queen in bed with her baby (Prince Edward), justifying its editorial decision by saying that the picture had already appeared in *Paris Match* and *Life*.

It was in such conditions of evolution and uncertainty that Buckingham Palace, unusually, seized the initiative. The Abominable No Man was succeeded as royal press secretary by William Heseltine, an Australian who applied very different standards to his relations with journalists: inviting them in, instead of keeping them out. As Commander Colville's assistant, Heseltine had already master-minded the public knighting of Francis Chichester, the round-the-world yachtsman, at Greenwich, as a television event. After his appointment, cameras were brought in for a royal banquet. '. . . [T]here is a distinct wind of change in the Palace', a bemused General Manager of BBC Outside Television Broadcasts minuted colleagues in July 1968. 'It has been growing in momentum over the last few months'.[14] The wind became a tornado in 1969 with the screening of *Royal Family*, a BBC documentary based on a fly-on-the-wall observation of the Queen at work and play over the course of a whole year, in anticipation of the Investiture of Charles as Prince of Wales at Carnaervon.

In addition to Heseltine, those closely involved included Prince Philip and Lord Mountbatten's son-in-law, the film director Lord Brabourne. The film was made by the head of BBC documentaries, Richard Cawston, and was presented as educational. In practice, it was a Buckingham Palace-inspired attempt to trump the gossip columnists and revive intelligent interest in royalty. The film showed the Queen as a sharp and vivacious person—not, as she was still widely regarded, a 'recent candidate for Confirmation'—and her family as busily engaged human beings. It succeeded beyond anybody's expectations, arousing enormous worldwide interest.

Against such a background, the once distant royals became all too familiar: the age of boredom became the age of stardom. One media event followed another. The Prince of Wales Investiture, viewed through a perspex canopy designed for the world's cameras, was a television spectacular, whose purpose—other than to capture attention by providing entertainment, with royals in the leading roles—was hard to discern. Before the Investiture, Charles was interviewed on the radio. Soon, almost every minor royal had appeared on a chat show. Anne, a talented show jumper, became sports personality of the year. The sense of royalty as flesh-and-blood celebrities intensified: Charles was kiss-chased across Australian beaches by blondes in bikinis. Nor were such attentions regarded as unwelcome. On the contrary, royalty was frequently congratulated for its mastery of television, and for its modern approach.

The problem was one of substance. The royals were now as famous as they had ever been and as popular. But famous and popular for what? Sport? The Navy? Good works? Sex appeal? Being royal? As one huge, expensive, conspicuously-consumptive marriage of a minor royal—Margaret, Anne, Charles and Andrew—followed another, the unanswerable question became more pressing. Most of the traditional roles of the constitutional Monarchy— imperial, political, constitutional, social—had either disappeared, or had shrunk to a point at which they no longer, in themselves, justified or explained the institution's high profile.

Increasingly, therefore, royal image-makers, and press commentators on royalty, resorted to an implicit message of the Cawston film: the Windsors were not only a Royal Family, but a Model Family as well, not just the symbol of the family life many subjects aspired to, but a living embodiment of it. The royals, in short, deserved to be revered because, in their affection for one another and enjoyment of each other's company, as in their active, prosper-ous, healthy lives and their devotion to public duty, they were a model to us all.

The notion of the Royal Family as a family of families in a literal sense received warm support from politicians and churchmen, and from the public which—at a time when unmodel families were becoming more common— wanted to believe it. It was, however, a perilous one. While the bull market in royal adulation continued, and the inner royals enjoyed visibly robust private lives, it could be sustained easily enough. But it was a hostage to fortune— partly because there was no genetic or any other reason why royals should be more model than anybody else and indeed (as Walter Bagehot once pointed out), the temptations confronting them made them less likely to be so; and partly because the press was becoming increasingly intrusive in its investiga-tions of the private lives of public figures in general.

Diana

Just as the age of British Shintoism, having peaked at the Coronation and in the 1953-4 Commonwealth tour, drifted into an anti-climactic malaise, so the age of stardom reached a climax with the marriage of the Prince and Princess of Wales in 1981, and—having offered heightened expectation—left the public unfulfilled. What had the marriage been for? With hindsight, it is possible to see what should have been evident at the time: in particular, the intensity of the media pressure, and the world's collusion in make-believe. For anybody, at such a private moment, the strain would have been hard to bear. For an uneducated, inexperienced and uncounselled adolescent from a broken home given to depression, it amounted to abuse. If the media are criticised now, they should have been criticised far more then: not so much for their intrusiveness, as for their slavish willingness to take everything on trust.

The writer Jan Morris was a rare exception. 'I would like to put on record, in *The Times* of July 29, 1981', she wrote, in a published letter, 'one citizen's sense of revulsion and foreboding at the ostentation, the extravagance and the sycophancy surrounding today's wedding of the heir to the British throne'. Nobody took any notice. Six hundred thousand people lined the route, and a billion watched the theatrical production at home. 'The Royal Family of England pulls off ceremonies the way the army of Israel pulls off commando raids', observed the *Boston Globe*. The face of Diana, her hairstyle, her movements and gestures, became the best known in the world.

In the case of Diana, deification was almost instant: but—in contrst to the mood surrounding Princess Elizabeth at a similar age—it was not combined with automatic admiration, or even unqlified respect. From the start, there was a hounding of the Princess of Wales of a kind that had never taken place before. When public desire is aroused to the extent that it occurred over the Charles-Diana wedding, it cannot be switched off, like a tap, simply because that is the convenient thing for those on the receiving end. Thus the story of Palace relations with the press after 1981 is one of rapid souring, as royal requests for restraint were met with incomprehension by tabloid editors for whom the competitive dredge for royalty sensation was simply business. Critically, in this period, there was a shift: the age of stardom became the age of pillorying, and of ridicule. Reporting of Princess Margaret's defiant romance with the landscape gardener Roddy Llewellyn in the 1970s had already paved the way. In the 1980s, the traditional press belief that as many readers would be put off as would be attracted by royal scandal was turned round: and the search was on for dirt.

In the new conditions, the rat-tat exchange of press 'revelations' and Palace condemnations of them became an established procedure. Replenishments to the royal finances served as a justification or excuse for people who sought to argue that a family so heavily supported out of public funds had little right to personal privacy anyway. The Monarch was impregnable on personal grounds. She also aroused much less interest and received far less coverage than the younger generation of royals. However, as the style of reporting and commentary changed—as obsequiousness gave way to cheeky familiarity and thence to vulgar teasing—so the last remaining citadels of royal immunity became vulnerable.

The question of how much money the Monarch had and needed, and what she should be expected to do with it, had cropped up as a news item in the early 1970s, when rapid inflation had forced the Palace to seek a revision of the Civil List, and a Select Committee had been set up to scrutinise the royal request. The Head of State was awarded her pay rise (as the tabloid press liked to describe it), but one of the outcomes had been to draw attention to the unrevealed royal fortune, and the Queen's right not to pay tax. The idea of the Monarch as tight-fisted, and the discovery that a majority of newspaper readers felt that she was overpaid for what she did, encouraged editors to probe deeper every time further requests for additional income were made. Thus an area of acceptable attack was gradually established, and the once inviolable Sovereign came to be seen as a legitimate target. By the 1990s, lampoons of the Queen were everywhere. On television—the medium that had once been refused permission to take close-up pictures of the Monarch's face—caricaturists regularly entertained viewers with a merciless *Spitting Image* 'Queen' puppet.

The new savagery spread up from the tabloids and sideways from *Private Eye*, to the broadsheets. For a long time, the latter had been divided between those that continued to provide semi-reverential copy, and those that regarded royalty as too trivial to discuss, except when the tabloids got a really good scoop. Circulation wars, together with an ever-rising tide of public interest in a model family's increasing propensity for gaffes and questionable behaviour, caused even the stuffiest papers to adopt new policies.

The Murdoch press was important here. During the 1980s, the ever-enterprising *Sun*, closely followed by the *Sunday Times*, communicated to their readership their indifference to royal claims to special treatment, and gained circulation as a result. It was Kelvin MacKenzie, of the *Sun*, who pioneered the tabloid habit of supplying a dose of royalty as part of a regular diet, regardless of whether there was anything new to say. 'Give me a Sunday for Monday splash on the royals', MacKenzie reputedly instructed his staff. 'Don't worry if it's not true—so long as there's not too much fuss about it afterwards'.[15] In 1986, Andrew Neil, maverick editor of the *Sunday Times*, provoked political uproar and caused Palace embarrassment with a story (which had some basis in fact) that the Queen and Mrs Thatcher were at loggerheads over government policy, especially towards South Africa.

But it was not, of course, just the press. In their different ways, the Queen's two daughters-in-law turned media intrusiveness on its head: chased by newsmen, they alternatively complained about their attentions and took them into their confidence. Yet another phase was entered when, in 1992, the *Sunday Times* serialised Andrew Morton's *Diana: Her True Story*. There was more to come: when, in the same year, the *Mirror* ran the Fergie toe-sucking pictures, the *Sun* retaliated with the Squidgy tape, confirming Morton's account of Diana's unhappiness. As royal marriages tumbled one by one, the Windsor Castle fire—and a sharply hostile public reaction to a Government promise to foot the bill—added to the sense of what the Queen, in a famous speech, called her *annus horribilis* ('One's Bum Year', punned the *Sun*).

The year ended with MacKenzie breaking the embargo on the Queen's Christmas broadcast.

Annus horribilis was not the end. Long before the discovery of the extent of Diana's involvement in the Morton book, a perception that royal reticence had become royal exhibitionism was strengthened by Prince Charles's own retaliatory revelations. Jonathan Dimbleby's biography of the Prince was originally envisaged, both by author and apparently by its subject, as a serious account of the Heir's life and work; the Prince's appalling frankness (including a televised admission of adultery) turned it into a salvo in the Charles-Diana war, and a feasting ground for the media. Virtually no interest was taken in Dimbleby's careful account of Prince Charles's charitable and other projects. Attention focused, instead, on paragraphs which seemed to suggest that the Queen was a cold and distant mother, that her husband was a bullying father, and that Diana was an uncontrollable manic depressive and hysteric.

The Waleses remained married until a media event made any continuation of their formal union an embarrassment. In November 1995, the Princess agreed to take part in an hour-long Panorama interview. It was a mark of how far the BBC had travelled since the days of Altrincham and Muggeridge that it even contemplated such an interview, quite apart from screening it without telling the Palace until an hour and a half before the official announcement. It was also the signal for the Palace to end its special relationship with the BBC. In the broadcast, the Princess replied to the Prince's confession with one of her own, and declared to a gigantic world audience her estranged husband's unfitness to be King. Afterwards, the media continued to be the arena for royal internecine warfare: the Queen's suggestion to both partners that they should conclude a divorce, was swiftly leaked to the press. A short time later, the Palace reacted to the BBC Panorama coup by coldly announcing the end of the BBC monopoly over the royal Christmas broadcast.

The sudden death of Diana, Princess of Wales, on 31 August 1997 dramatically altered the media approach to royalty in a variety of ways. Before it, Diana's romantic life continued to provide the tabloids with their daily fare, while Charles sank perilously low in the public esteem, partly because of his refusal to hide his relationship with Camilla Parker-Bowles. Coverage of the Princess was by no means wholly sympathetic. There were whispers that Diana, approaching middle-age, could not continue to be portrayed in the media as a wayward siren for ever, and jokes were made about the Princess, on holiday in France, walking long distances in a skimpy bathing-suit in order to tell photographers to stop bothering her. It was not until after her death that the world discovered how far sixteen or so years of daily news reporting had branded her face, style, clothes, mannerisms—and also her Panorama-exposed personality—onto its consciousness.

The scale of the public grief—from Bangkok to Los Angeles, Glasgow to the Philippines—was an unprecedented tribute to an individual. It was also a new and startling demonstration of the ability of the global media to universalise. Yet, if the media created the legend, and if the deification of Diana can be seen as a frightening by-product of modern technology, there was also a key ingredient that had nothing to do with newsprint or the electronic image.

Though divorced, though self-confessedly adulterous, though no longer a Royal Highness, Diana remained, and was perceived as being, 'royal'. The story of the media-Palace nexus has been fast-rolling, as old assumptions have been discarded, and deference turned into something close to contempt. What has not changed is the mainspring of royalty stories and icons: the public's fascination with kings, queens, princes, princesses, their employees, friends and lovers, and how they live their lives. The discovery of the last quarter of the twentieth century has been that an increasingly egalitarian, socially-integrated, and racially-mixed population becomes more interested, not less.

How far is this interest, in itself, media-generated? Since the Monarchy and media are today so closely enmeshed, it has become hard—as it was under different circumstances during the Second World War—to draw a line between fantasy and reality. Indeed, it has become impossible to imagine modern royalty except in the context of a spotlight: if being royal once meant crowns and orbs and people bowing and walking backwards, at the end of the twentieth century it means the omnipresence of 'those awful lights', along with telescopic lenses and official denials. Royal protestations about excessive media attention should be seen in this context. So should any simply blaming of the media for the Monarchy's troubles: the daily diet of royal entertainment would quickly diminish if there were a lagging demand for it. Presumably press stories about the British Royal Family will eventually abate. That they show little sign of doing so a year after the death of Diana reflects a continuing public obsession. Indeed, if the media made possible the state of mind that led to the 'ocean of flowers', there is plenty of evidence of the spontaneity of the tributes, and of the press being taken aback by what occurred.

Shrug

Will the Monarchy-media symbiosis end in the Monarchy's suffocation? The possibility cannot be ruled out. We do not yet know the feelings of Prince William and Prince Harry on the subject of their own future careers, though William is believed to be camera-shy, which does not bode well for a lifetime in the public gaze. Sooner or later, the strains on the institution and its central personalities may persuade a Monarch or Heir simply to walk away from arbitrarily imposed responsibilities with a dismissive and defiant shrug—as Edward VIII did in 1936, and as Margaret appeared to do several decades later. If that happens, the impact of the media—on private lives, on the difficulty of conducting normal relationships—must surely be regarded as a factor. At the same time, of course, royal news has had its effect on the media:

trivialising news broadcasts, distorting agendas, squeezing out or dumbing down serious discussion.

Finally, will history regard the twentieth century Monarchy myth as peripheral? Will the Diana-mourning be seen as a blip, or a symptom? Up till now, most serious analysts have pushed the inconvenient phenomenon of modern royalty on one side, and have treated the reporting of it as not only kitsch, but trivial. Perhaps they are wrong to do so. Indeed it is arguable that recent events point to a central place in popular feeling, and hence a role in political and social relationships, which cannot be ignored; and that the alchemy of media-plus-monarchy is potentially an explosive, as well as mystifying, one.

Biographical Note

Ben Pimlott is Warden of Goldsmiths' College, University of London, and author of *The Queen: A Biography of Elizabeth II*.

Notes

1 Toronto, John C. Winston Co. Ltd, p. 127.
2 *Saturday Evening Post*, 19.10.57.
3 *The Magic of Monarchy*, London, T. Nelson & Sons, 1937, p. 11.
4 12.12.36 Beatrice Webb Diary; eds., N. and J. Mackenzie, *The Wheel of Life: The Diary of Beatrice Webb*, Vol. 4, 1924–1943, London, Virago, 1985, p. 382.
5 G. Dennis, *Coronation Commentary*, New York, Dodd, Mead and Co., 1937, p. 201.
6 HRH Princess Elizabeth, 'The Coronation, 12 May 1937' (Royal Library, Windsor).
7 *The Strenuous Years: Diaries 1948–1955*, London, Weidenfeld and Nicolson, 1973, p. 147.
8 *The Modern British Monarchy*, London, Eyre and Spottiswoode, 1961, p. 26.
9 *Strenuous Years*, p. 114.
10 'The Monarchy Today', *National and English Review*, August 1957, p. 67.
11 *Saturday Evening Post*, 19.10.57.
12 'Some Further Points on the Muggeridge Incident', Grisewood to Sir Ian Jacob, 23.10.57, BBC Written Archives (Caversham).
13 3.12.58, Anthony Craxton memo, T16/186/5, BBC Written Archives (Caversham).
14 16.7.68, T16/186/8, BBC Written Archives (Caversham).
15 P. Chippendale and C. Horrie, *Stick It Up Your Punter! The Rise and Fall of the Sun*, London, Heinemann, 1990, p. 106.

Judging the Media: Impartiality and Broadcasting

ERIC BARENDT

EVERYONE knows now that elections are won by the press. After all, the *Sun* itself claimed credit for the surprise victory of the Conservatives in the General Election of 1992, and the Party Treasurer at the time, Lord MacAlpine (subsequently a supporter of the Referendum Party), paid tribute to the tabloids for their help. Tony Blair in opposition assiduously courted Rupert Murdoch and the editors of his newspapers. It is unlikely that the Labour majority in 1997 would have been so large, had the *Sun* not decided to support it six weeks before polling day. Newspapers are, of course, free to support whichever party its editor, or proprietor, chooses, and to take sides on political issues. Nobody expects them to be impartial or balanced in their coverage of contentious political matters such as participation in European Economic and Monetary Union or welfare reform, or in their treatment of industrial disputes. These freedoms are essential aspects of our traditional understanding of 'press freedom', constitutionally guaranteed in many countries, notably in the USA by the First Amendment.

In contrast, television and radio are required by law to be impartial in their treatment of political and industrial controversies. Further, it is impermissible for broadcasters to 'editorialise' on these matters. The requirement to show 'due impartiality' has been imposed by statute on the private sector since its inception in 1954, but was only incorporated in the BBC Licence in 1996; previously the Corporation had accepted the obligation voluntarily. Not only the BBC, but every commercial television and radio licensee from Granada, Carlton and Channel 4 to the most modest community station, is debarred from taking political sides. These principles apply to the coverage of elections, and to the allocation of political and election broadcasts, matters of great controversy in the recent General Election. The constraints may irritate individual broadcasting journalists and producers from time to time; but most broadcasters, and certainly their regulators, accept and live with them. The impartiality principle and the ban on editorialising are part of the culture of control which has governed broadcasting since the 1920s.

But it is reasonable to question whether this degree of control is now appropriate in a multi-channel environment. Moreover, this article will argue that in practice the application of the impartiality principle leaves much to the judgment of the broadcasting companies themselves. The Independent Television Commission (ITC) and Radio Authority cannot now intervene before programmes are broadcast, and are reluctant to hold the broadcasters to account subsequently. Further, the courts have also generally been unwilling to intervene in this area. An application for judicial review will only be successful if there is a plain breach of the impartiality rule. The implications of this reluctance on the part of both regulatory authorities and the courts will be considered in the final part of the article.

Why impartiality in broadcasting?

It is obviously right that public broadcasters should be impartial in their treatment of political questions, just as it is reasonable to require them to put on serious current affairs and arts programmes to fulfil their 'public service' remit to inform, educate and entertain. Licence fee payers cannot be expected to support politically biased channels. But it is far from clear that the same duties should be imposed on private commercial channels, particularly in an environment where the public has access to more than a handful of them. Admittedly at the moment, many viewers only receive two or three commercial television channels, but that is not the case with subscribers to satellite or cable television. With the imminent advent of digital terrestrial television, viewers will be able to choose between 30 or so channels without subscribing to satellite or cable services. Moreover, the present numerical shortage of television channels hardly applies to radio; but the impartiality principle applies as much to the older medium as it does to television, albeit in a slightly diluted form for local stations. They must not give undue prominence to any political views or parties.

In other countries, similar rules have been scrapped, or at least modified in the context of commercial broadcasting. The United States Federal Communications Commission (FCC) repealed its Fairness Doctrine in 1987; the Doctrine had required all broadcasters, radio and television, to devote a proportion of their programme schedules to the treatment of controversial issues and to discuss them in an even-handed and balanced way.

Although the Doctrine had been upheld in 1969 by the Supreme Court, as compatible with the First Amendment freedom of speech, the FCC decided it was unnecessary in view of the proliferation of terrestrial and cable channels. In its opinion, the market should ensure that views not presented on one channel would find a place on another. This perception is of course open to question, but it is taken for granted in the newspaper and magazine world.

In some European countries, a more relaxed view of balance and impartiality is taken in the case of private channels. The range of programmes and views expressed on one channel is to be considered in conjunction with the schedules of the others. This is known as 'external pluralism', to be compared with the 'internal pluralism' or balance required of the public channels. But every television channel in the UK must be impartial. Internal pluralism is as required of Channel 4 and BSkyB as it is of the BBC.

It may, however, be wrong to regard the impartiality principle as a negative constraint on the freedom of broadcasters to draw up their own schedules and to express their own views. The Annan Committee which considered the broadcasting landscape in 1977 regarded it rather as an encouragement to the presentation of dissenting or radical views and the scheduling of programmes of interest to minority groups. This perspective applies as much to politics as it does to arts and social affairs programmes. Current affairs programme and documentaries must give some time to the expression of minority views and to representatives of the smaller political parties, such as the Greens, unrepresented in Parliament. To some extent this perspective on the impartiality rule is captured by the distinctive remit of Channel 4: it must schedule programmes which 'appeal to tastes and interests not generally catered for' on the principal commercial channel, Channel 3.

Although these points have some merit, it is now difficult to find convincing arguments to justify the imposition of a rigorous impartiality standard on private commercial broadcasters, when none is applied to the print media. Perhaps the best argument is one of tradition; we are accustomed in Britain, as in other European countries, to the political bias of newspapers, but we expect radio and television to cover news and political disputes fairly and objectively.

If the impartiality and no-editorialising rules were lifted, the broadcasting media might more or less uniformly swing behind the Conservative party, just as the vast majority of the national press, until recently, has favoured the political right. Interestingly, however, the impartiality rule was tightened a little in the Broadcasting Act 1990 in order to counteract what the Thatcher government perceived as the left-wing prejudices of most broadcasters. The ITC was required to produce a Code, setting out, for instance, when it was appropriate to require balance within an individual programme instead of over a series of programmes. The Code, the latest version of which was issued in 1995, makes it clear, among other requirements, that each channel must be impartial; it cannot point to balancing programme on other channels. 'Personal view' programmes may be allowed, but they must be followed by a studio discussion of the issues or the presentation of a reply from a different political perspective.

Impartiality and politics

In assessing the coherence of the impartiality rule in the context of party politics, a distinction should be drawn between the broadcasters' own programmes, such as *Panorama* or *World in Action*, on the one hand, and the party political and election broadcasts on the other. Legislation now makes explicit provision for the latter. The Broadcasting Act 1990, section 36, authorises the ITC to decide which parties are entitled to make these broadcasts, and their length and frequency. In practice, the allocation is made in consultation with the BBC and the major political parties represented in Parliament, but the ITC has the last word, at least as far as Channels 3, 4 and 5 are concerned. (Satellite and cable channels are not required to transmit the

parties' broadcasts, but they are, of course, required to show 'due impartiality' in their coverage, if any, of political issues.)

As far as the broadcasters' own news, documentary and current affairs
programmes are concerned, the impartiality rule may on occasion require a
particular programme to be balanced in its treatment. The BBC, for instance,
breached the rule when in the spring of 1995 three days before the Scottish
local elections it proposed to devote an edition of *Panorama* to an interview
with the Prime Minister, John Major.[1] Members of the Scottish National Party
succeeded in their application for an interdict to stop the transmission; the
court was unimpressed by the argument that the SNP had enjoyed equivalent
exposure in other news and current affairs programmes.

Arguably, the *Panorama* case was straightforward. It can hardly satisfy
impartiality for a broadcaster to give the leader of one party such exposure in
its flagship political programme so soon before an election. In fact, it was one
of the very few cases in which the broadcasters' judgment, or lack of it, has
been overturned by the courts. The Scottish National Party, always an active
litigant, has been less successful in other cases. In 1996 it failed in a challenge
to the BBC's allocation of time for the coverage of the party conferences, under
which the three major UK parties were given much more generous treatment
(18 hours for the Labour party, 17 for the Conservatives, and 13 for the
Liberals) than the SNP which only got 5 hours of coverage. One reason for the
decision was that the BBC, and other broadcasters, enjoy substantial discretion in determining how to apply the requirement of 'due impartiality'
imposed by the BBC Licence and the Broadcasting Act 1990.[2]

'Due impartiality' does not mean absolute equality of treatment, but
fairness. The courts will only interfere with the broadcasting authorities'
judgment when it is plainly wrong: what is termed in the language of
administrative law an abuse of discretion or an irrational judgment. Moreover, as I will explain later, there are other obstacles to effective judicial
intervention in this area.

The SNP was also unsuccessful when it tried to challenge the broadcasters' plans to stage a head to head debate between the major party
leaders before the May election in 1997. The plans were abortive, largely, it is
conjectured, because the Labour Party thought it unwise to jeopardise its
electoral lead in the polls by agreeing to a confrontation between John Major
and Tony Blair. It was unclear whether the debate would also have involved
Paddy Ashdown, but two Scottish channels, Scottish TV and Grampian,
admitted it would not feature the SNP leader, Alex Salmond. That was the
occasion for the litigation. The judge dismissed the case, largely on the
ground that it was premature to bring it before the debate had been firmly
scheduled.[3] But he also accepted the broadcasters' argument that impartiality should be assessed in this context over the whole range of election
programmes; the SNP leader would appear in other programmes, which
would balance his omission from the proposed debate between the two (or
possibly three) national party leaders. This conclusion can be questioned.

Arguably, participation in a debate between party leaders is more important than exposure in other programmes. The point, however, is that it is difficult to determine exactly what 'due impartiality' really means in this context. Further, there is a question of institutional competence here: it is unclear whether it is more appropriate for the broadcasting authorities or the courts to decide the matter.

In fact, very few cases are taken to the courts. Outside the area of election campaigns, complainants are almost always happy to leave the matter with the ITC and the Radio Authority. Alternatively, they can complain to the Broadcasting Standards Commission, previously in this context the Complaints Commission, on the ground that they have received 'unjust or unfair treatment'.[4] Impartiality complaints make up only a small proportion of the number of complaints made to the ITC: in 1995, 65 out of 4,507, in 1996, 95 out of 2,724. Many more complaints are made about matters of taste and decency, or general accuracy.

It is clearly difficult for broadcasters to get things right when it comes to interviewing the Prime Minister. In July 1996 the Labour Party complained that the ITN News at Ten had breached the impartiality requirement by scheduling an interview with John Major as a leading item when this was not part of any planned sequence of interviews with all the party leaders; further, it alleged that the newscaster, Trevor McDonald, had created too cosy and friendly an atmosphere. The ITC rejected both complaints. Broadly, each party leader had enjoyed comparable amounts of news time and prominence over the past year; but it did suggest that some viewers might have found McDonald's overall approach in the interview too relaxed. Earlier in the year, the Commission had also rejected a complaint that an interview with Major on the Meridian regional news programme about the BSE scare had been too hostile and so breached the impartiality principle, though again it found shortcomings in the style and approach of the interview. Complaints arising from an interview of Sir James Goldsmith of the Referendum Party by Jonathan Dimbleby were also rejected, on the ground that the interviewer's approach had been 'firm' rather than 'rude'.

The reluctance of the ITC to intervene in cases of this kind may not necessarily show that the impartiality requirement is valueless. It does set standards and reminds broadcasters and interviewers that they must comply with minimum standards of courtesy and firmness. The Commission is rightly reluctant to intervene by holding that the requirement has been broken, with the possibility of a formal warning to, or even the imposition of a fine on, the company concerned. The possibility of such sanctions might cramp broadcasters by making them anxious not to offend their interviewees. They might be reluctant to question politicians firmly, and the end result would be a dumbing-down of the quality of current affairs and political programmes. Further, schedulers might be induced to adopt a stop-watch approach to ensure that party leaders and spokesmen were given exactly equal or proportionate exposure.

The Broadcasting Complaints Commission, now the Standards Commission, has also been reluctant to intervene with the broadcasters' judgment about the appropriate amount of time to allocate to the political parties in their news and current affairs coverage. When the leaders of the (then independent) Liberal and Social Democrat parties complained to the Commission that they had received 'unfair treatment' in comparison with the Labour Party over a two month period subsequent to the General Election of 1983, the Commission ruled that it was inappropriate for it to consider a political complaint about the amount of coverage over a range of programmes, as distinct from a particular programme. David Owen challenged this decision in the courts, but it was upheld.[5] The Divisional Court ruled that the Commission was entitled in a matter of this political sensitivity to leave the allocation of coverage to the broadcasters themselves; the companies could reasonably take the view that the Labour Party was entitled to greater coverage as it was the official Opposition, having won many more seats, if not votes, at the 1983 Election.

The allocation of election broadcasts

The impartiality principle also applies to the allocation of election and regular party political broadcasts. As already mentioned, the ITC has final responsibility in the commercial sector for their allocation, if this is not amicably agreed between the parties. For General Election broadcasts, allocation is determined by reference to each party's electoral support in the previous General Election and the number of candidates it intends to field; each party putting up at least 50 candidates is guaranteed one broadcast on television of five minutes.

It is, of course, questionable whether these criteria are the most appropriate means for ensuring 'due impartiality' in the election context. Their application to particular cases may also be controversial. For a start, it seems the criteria attach no importance to the performance of the party in the European or local elections which will, most probably, have been held since the previous General Election. Secondly, it may be wrong to attach much weight to the number of candidates fielded by the party. As the Referendum Party showed at last year's election, it is quite easy for someone as rich as Goldsmith to finance a large number of candidates, none of whom, it was agreed, had any chance of getting elected. Perhaps it would be better to focus on the party's membership, the duration of its existence, and other indications of its possible potency as a serious political force.

The application of these criteria has been challenged in the courts twice, on each occasion unsuccessfully. In 1987, SNP leaders challenged the decision of the Independent Broadcasting Authority (the predecessor of the ITC) to allocate it two broadcasts, while the three major parties, the Conservatives, Labour, and the Liberal-SDP Alliance were given five overall, of which two had a Scottish focus. The SNP argued that it should have the same number of broadcasts as the three United Kingdom parties, on the basis of its local electoral success in the two preceding years and the number of candidates it was fielding. Viewed from a Scottish nationalist perspective this may have seemed a reasonable case; but Lord Prosser rejected the challenge, on the basis that the IBA was entitled to take account of the United Kingdom dimension. The other three parties were contesting seats throughout the UK, and all claimed to have a chance of forming the government after the election. The SNP could not claim that.

Last year the Referendum Party challenged its allocation of only one five minute broadcast. It argued that, as it was fielding 547 candidates in the 659 constituencies, it should have been treated more generously. The Divisional Court rejected the challenge on the ground that the broadcasting authorities' decision could not be characterised as so irrational or grossly unreasonable as to warrant judicial review.[6] The Referendum Party contended that it was wrong for the BBC and ITC to take past electoral support into account in this context, when the party was a new one which had not existed at the time of the previous election. The Court agreed it would have been wrong for the authorities to treat this criterion as decisive; but they were entitled to determine the weight to be put on the number of candidates fielded by the applicants and other indications of electoral support. They had listened to the party's arguments, and there was no evidence that they had reached the decision irrationally.

Earlier I criticised the relevance of the number of candidates as a criterion for allocating election broadcasts. But insofar as it is a valid criterion, it is hard to see what ground the broadcasting authorities could have had for denying the Referendum Party, fighting well over three quarters of the seats, more generous treatment than, say, the British National Party and the Pro-Life Alliance Party. Both of these parties just crossed the 50 candidate threshold, and were given the same broadcasting time as the Referendum Party.

What emerges from these two cases is the difficulty of applying the impartiality requirement to the allocation of election broadcasts. It would be absurd to treat all parties equally, provided, say, they put forward a minimum number of candidates, but it is virtually impossible to say with precision what fairness requires. It is quite different in a referendum, when it is right to give equal time to both sides, that fighting for a YES vote and the NO campaign organisation. Secondly, the courts are as reluctant to interfere with the broadcasting authorities' discretion in this context as they are in other cases involving the application of the impartiality principle. Perhaps this is because of the political sensitivity of these decisions. The courts do not want to interfere in matters of party policies, unless this is absolutely unavoidable.

But another explanation for the courts' reluctance to question ITC discretion in applying the impartiality rule is to be found in the terms of the 1990 broadcasting legislation. The statute requires the ITC to do all it can to ensure that 'due impartiality' is complied with by licensees, such as Scottish

Television, Carlton, and Granada. The Commission, unlike its predecessor, the Independent Broadcasting Authority, has no power to intervene before programmes go out by previewing them or by directing the broadcasting company to revise its schedule to ensure balanced treatment. The ITC can only act retrospectively by admonishing or penalising the broadcaster for a breach of the impartiality provisions of the Code. Against that background, it would be difficult for a court to conclude the ITC has not done all it can to ensure balance and impartiality.

Conclusions

Application of the impartiality rule in the context of political broadcasting is bound to be controversial. This is particularly true with regard to the allocation of election broadcasts and the broadcast of programmes, such as debates between party leaders, held during the course of the campaign. Apart from referendum campaigns, it is far from clear what 'due impartiality' entails, even if it is translated into such terms as 'fairness' or 'balance'.

To some extent the application of the rule conceals interesting and contentious issues about the nature of elections: are they held primarily to choose a government or to elect members of the legislature? On the former interpretation, it is right to give much more coverage, and broadcasting opportunities, to the leaders of the two major parties than to spokesmen for the third and other parties. On the other perspective, it is fair to give minority parties and independent candidates ample opportunity to get their message across to the public. Secondly, emphasis on the vote the party received at a prior election may prejudice the formation of new parties and so fossilise the party system, while discounting that factor may encourage instability.

Another question is who, or which authority, should determine what constitutes impartiality. At the moment the ITC and Radio Authority lay down broad principles for its application, fleshing out the rudimentary requirements of the statute, the Broadcasting Act 1990. But in practice it is for the broadcasting companies, as well, of course, as the BBC, to determine how these principles are applied in the course, say, of an election campaign. Political parties and candidates cannot complain to the regulatory authority until the programme has gone out, for the authorities now have no power to scrutinise scheduling and programme decisions before transmission. Admittedly, the ITC determines the allocation of election broadcasts, though again it is for the broadcasting company to ensure that the party's broadcast complies with the law, including the requirements imposed by the broadcasting legislation itself.[7]

We have seen that the ITC is reluctant to reprimand the broadcasters afterwards, while the courts are unwilling to question how the Commission exercises its supervisory powers. There are, as mentioned, some understandable reasons for their caution: the authorities must balance concern for the enforcement of programme standards against undue interference with the broadcasting freedom of producers, which has a narrower scope than the freedom of newspaper editors and journalists. Against that, it may be undesirable to leave application of the impartiality rule to the broadcasters themselves. These decisions are sometimes very sensitive. Conceivably, they could have significant impact on the outcome of an election. Yet they may be taken by a commercial broadcaster, only accountable afterwards to a regulatory authority, which is reluctant to question the former's judgment.

In their turn, the courts prefer to leave matters to the judgment of the broadcasting authorities or the broadcasters. There may be good legal and prudential reasons for this course; the English judiciary has always been reluctant to become involved in media regulation. But the result is that decisions about impartiality in broadcasting are not subject to the full and searching scrutiny which is warranted and which they might receive if the courts were more active. That is a pity, because fairness in the media treatment of elections and in the allocation of party broadcasts is an integral aspect of the fairness of elections.

Biographical Note

Eric Barendt is the Goodman Professor of Media Law, University College London. He is the author of *Freedom of Speech* (1987) and *Broadcasting Law* (1995), both published by Oxford University Press.

Notes

1 *Houston* v. *BBC*, 1995 *Scottish Law Times* 1305.
2 See C. R. Munro, *New Law Journal*, 146, p. 1433.
3 See Munro, *New Law Journal*, 147, p. 528.
4 Broadcasting Act 1996, s. 110.
5 *R.* v. *Broadcasting Complaints Commission, ex parte Owen*, 1985, QB 1153.
6 *R.* v. *ITC, ex parte Referendum Party*, 1997, Crown Office Digest 459.
7 In the 1997 election campaign, broadcasters required changes to be made to the Election Broadcasts of the British National Party and of the Pro-Life Alliance. Complaints to the ITC about the content of the broadcasts were rejected.

A Fresh Look at Freedom of Speech

JEAN SEATON

LIBERAL democracy is not stable. It is not a thing. You cannot 'reach' it, or 'have' it. Like mist or water slipping through your fingers, it lacks a form: Loki the shape changer in Norse myth is perhaps the best metaphor. Democracy is different everywhere, and alters in nature over time. Its character is determined by how the franchise works, by the beneficiaries of the electoral process, by social and economic circumstances. Outside factors—in particular the ever-changing structure of civil society—determine its quality. So do the ever-evolving institutions of state, and the social and political environment, of which the modern mass media forms a critical part.

Indeed, the mass media are today an essential part of the climate in which democracy may languish or flourish. Consequently changes in the technology and the markets affecting the media influence much more than just the opportunity for politicians to communicate. They help to determine, and potentially to transform, the conditions in which a democracy can operate. There is a longstanding discussion about whether the media have quantifiable 'effects' on individuals: by contrast, the question of their impact on institutions frequently goes unremarked. Yet the reality is that the state of 'political' media—which provide the arena for so much of the political debate—closely reflect the conditions of the commercial market-place in which the media industries work.

The relationship between the press and politicians has always been interlocked, yet market driven. For example, just as one generation of party politicians discovered the scope for using a mass press to reach their public, cutting out much of the propagandist role of traditional parties, so the emergence of broadcasting later enabled party leaders to speak directly to the electorate, without any intermediary. Party structures developed alternative functions: as selectorates, ideological guardians, power bases. Political communication moved from the doorstep and the mass meeting to the media. The process was already far advanced in the age of radio; it has been taken immeasurably further by television. Today, the definition of political 'leadership' depends, to an extraordinary extent, on the capacity of a politician for self-projection on the screen.

College Green

There has been a geographical effect: in US and European politics, television has shifted the *location* of political happenings from legislatures and conference halls to where television discussions and interviews take place. A

© The Political Quarterly Publishing Co. Ltd. 1990
Published by Blackwell Publishers, 108 Cowley Road, Oxford OX4 1JF, UK and 350 Main Street, Malden, MA 02148, USA

product of the 1980s in Britain has been the development of a windswept triangle of grass called College Green, between the Houses of Parliament and the Millbank studios, as a nationally recognised platform, and part of the unwritten constitution. It is a very rule-governed triangle: it is understood, for example, that it is here that parliamentarians offer instant opinions about each other under the dominant broadcasting regulation of political balance. The sense of a parliamentary environment and backcloth—outside the House, but also outside a studio—offers a necessary informal intimacy and neutrality, before MPs rush back into the House. Indeed, so popular has this patch become that it has acquired the feeling of a semi-permanent encampment, and one which MPs would frequently prefer to the floor of the House itself.

College Green is a new, media-made public space. Meanwhile, the press have created, out of public politics, a newly privatised one. It is not just that we join less, combine less, and compete on our own more (as Robert Putnam has pointed out);[1] we go out less purposively, and are willing, and indeed may feel we have to, to spend more on what we do at home. People will pay a lot of money on entertainment technology that removes the need for them to leave their houses. 'Free speech' as a result operates under new conditions. Radio, television, the telephone, and now the worldwide web have provided an opportunity for real or spurious direct participation through 'phone-in' and—most recently—'vote-in' current affairs programmes.

Though the organisation of such programmes is designed for entertainment, political parties already acknowledge their ability to influence the climate of opinion and—though they may need more external scrutiny—their scope has become astonishingly wide. Not only is there a kind of 'plebiscitory' relationship between the mass public and poetry (voting for your favourite 'poem of the day'), you can also have your say on the Eurovision Song Contest, whether O. J. Simpson should have been convicted, and the future of the Monarchy. It is a short step, perhaps, from here to a system of constitutionally-sanctioned referenda on issues of serious national debate. Thus politics, always with an element of the blood sport, moves towards the ethics and psychology of the Roman arena, with a huge armchair audience enjoying the fighting for its own sake, and even having the thrill of a remote participation in the outcome.

'News as entertainment'—competing in the marketplace—provides, of course, the main basis for newspaper journalism. Until recently this did not necessarily preclude a rational consideration of current events. Thus, a growing readership for mass-market tabloids (in 1979 less than 40 per cent of British voters read a tabloid, by 1993 nearly 80 per cent did so), combined its consumption of simplified newspaper slogans with a diet of television news services whose content was determined by quality-newspaper values. However, that situation is changing, largely because of the market and a reluctance to interfere with it: a proliferation of channels, and the granting of franchises to companies with little 'public service' incentive, has been driving much of the serious coverage of politics on television in a tabloid direction.

118

What we have come to see in the last decade is a division in the electronic media similar to the one that already exists for print journalism: popular programmes for the masses in which news values are degraded, and high quality serious programmes (BBC2's *Newsnight* is a prime example) which neither expect nor obtain more than a small and specialised minority of viewers. There is a growing voluntary apartheid here which did not previously exist, and one with alarming implications for our democracy: the gap between the richest and the poorest, employed and unemployed, educated and uneducated, may come to be measured not just by differences in health and opportunities, but by an increasing polarisation of degrees of knowledge and understanding of current issues and political debates.

Media Immunities

Usually, in the past, because of their acknowledged role as the informing network for the citizenry in an open society, the media and their products have been permitted privileges that marked them out from other industries, goods and services. In some countries, protection for such privileges has been constitutionally sanctioned, as in the First Amendment of the US Constitution, which declares 'that Congress shall pass no Act that will abridge the freedom of speech'. On this basis, the American media have been accorded rights the interpretation of which have kept the courts busy and lawyers rich. Some such rights have been negative: preventing others from acting against the holders of the right. Others are determined by the limitations put on laws governing libel, economic competition, obscenity and official secrets, based on the claim of proprietors, editors and journalists that they publish in the public interest.

The nature of the privileges accorded to the press have varied. Sometimes they have been straightforwardly economic: for example, in recent British history, the exemption of books and periodicals from VAT. More far-reaching has been the monopoly position given to public broadcasting, and then the regulation of access to scarce air waves given to commercial undertakings in exchange for their management in the name of the public interest and political impartiality. In short, the media have been treated as a special case in the market: they have not been exposed to full competitive pressures, generally on the grounds that their political importance merited protection.

The sediment of rights and privileges on which the media in democratic countries are commonly based, and the arguments that have accrued in defence of them, have had mixed results and varied interpretations. Indeed, sometimes things have not turned out as intended, or as understood. For example, when, in the aftermath of the Second World War, the US government triumphantly and energetically pressed for Freedom of Information Exchange treaties throughout the western world, its overt aim was the liberal one of ensuring that there should be no quotas or bans on the exchange of cultural material. The consequence of this protected freedom was American domination of the market, and the collapse of independent national film industries across Europe. In this case, 'privilege', apparently, intended to be international, benefited one nation; but the principle that the media should be given a distinct status was accepted internationally on ideological grounds.

There was an implicit deal: media immunities were exchanged for the right of politicians to be heard, while simultaneously being scrutinised by the media they protected. The media existed, so it was understood, to rummage about in government, providing the public with uncensored information and explanation; but they were also there for politicians to communicate with and through. The arrangement, however, depended on conditions that have always been, and are today increasingly, insecure. Just as it is impossible to imagine a democracy without effective media scrutiny of government, so democracy is dependent on the ability of leaders, parties, and institutions to speak directly, and in a way in which they can expect to be listened to and heeded, to the people. Both have long involved an element of suspending disbelief: in practice, media scrutiny has only ever been partial, and much of the population has been oblivious to or uninterested in the pronouncements of leaders.

Modern conditions, however, conspire both to make the ability of journalists to get at, understand and communicate the reality of what is going on harder; while leaders struggle to get even a fraction of the public's cluttered attention. While governments are able to evade responsibility for much of what happens, political communication becomes less and less based on information, and more on the ingredients of image-making. In the process, policy becomes 'media-driven': the business of government is constantly interrupted by an inexorable pressure to get a political message across in over-simplified terms. Thus, successful ministers cease to be those who solve policy problems or negotiate effectively, but those with a good media rapport.

Yet at the same time the market place is full of media organisations competing for the public's favour, and—frequently—abandoning depth and objectivity in their analysis of politics in the pursuit of it. Reliability declines, newspapers chase political fashion instead of seeking to shape it.[2] (Interestingly, during the recent British election the editor of the *Sun* was limpidly frank about the process of deciding which party it would support: it would back, he announced, whichever party its proprietor told it to. Mr Murdoch, in turn, seems to have been influenced as much by a perception that in 1997, few readers of his tabloid sympathised with the Conservative government, as by hopes of corporate favours from a Labour one.)

Flowers

Partly *because* there are more media outlets today than there used to be, the authority of all has suffered a kind of dilution: there is no single paper (like *The Times*) or radio or TV station (BBC Radio 4, or BBC1), as in the past, from which the nation can take its cue, and derive a communally shared 'Establishment' approach to events. Instead there is a cacophony, not of variously opposed points of view, but of similar ones, all seeking to corner the same imagined waveband of public taste. Where, in the past, media reading, watching or listening was a way of participating, today it has become a form of consuming: the citizen takes one packet or another down from the shelf. Each has a different label, but the contents are virtually identical. Thus, it was scarcely coincidence that on polling day 1997, the *Mirror* and the *Sun*— previously political as well as commercial rivals and opponents—should have come up, independently, with identical front-page headlines.

There is a paradox: a great expansion in apparent opportunities (both for the citizen, and the professional politician, journalist or broadcaster) to communicate combined with tight real-world constraints: a thousand flowers blooming with (as it were) tightly bound feet. Not only do the messages the new media produce have a disconcerting similarity one with another: their presentation, shape, style is increasingly tied to rules and conventions. The reality, as everybody knows, is that most important political problems are complicated and many are increasingly technical: the pressures of the media inevitably gloss over anything that cannot be immediately understood.

The explanation is, of course, to be found in the nature of the media's other life: as industries increasingly placed on the margins of a vast, rapidly evolving entertainment business, whose boundaries are melting all the time. Some small-readership 'quality' papers have secured a temporary immunity as tiny parasites on the back of lumbering giants: their apparent security, however, is an illusion. Others have been exposed to the full blast of the global economy.

Already the newspapers have had to re-invent themselves, as more people get news from television. As recently as 1983, survey evidence suggested that while 60 per cent of the population acquired their knowledge of foreign news primarily from TV, as many as 28 per cent still did so from newspapers: a decade later, equivalent figures had shifted to 69 per cent and 19.5 per cent. There are carts and horses here: however, whether it has been cause or effect, or a mixture of the two, there has been a steady decline in newspaper reporting of news. While the quality press has turned from news to explanation and comment, the popular press had replaced news with scandal, sport, and sport involving scandal—plus a number of other staples like royalty, soap stars, and the paranormal. A time traveller from the Tudor period would recognise the tabloids as direct relations of his own sixteenth century 'fantasticle tales'. If, so far, the broadcasting media have yet to follow the same pattern, the signs are there, as demand for hard news on serious topics shrinks: tabloid telly is on its way.

Gluts

It is not just a question of consumer demand for news, or the lack of it. The lifeblood of the media industries that deal with politics most directly is

advertising revenue. Though newspapers and television are ostensibly concerned with the importance of the messages they convey to readers, their
commercial concern involves a different product and clientele: their first job is
to sell audiences to advertisers. The British and North European advertising
industry is sophisticated and segmented, with a highly-developed market,
though scarcely yet a transnational or pan-European one.

In Britain, advertising revenues have increased in the last decade as a
proportion of GDP, but with little of the additional earnings ploughed back
into newspapers. Most of it has gone on broadcasting,[3] which, in turn, creates
new problems. The proliferation of broadcasting opportunities presents
advertisers with a more fragmented audience, and hence a less attractive
one from an advertising point of view. Where costs of TV advertising have
fallen, thereby reducing the cost and quality of programmes—as in parts of
southern Europe—an opposite tendency has occurred, also with deleterious
effects: cheap TV advertising has led to advertising gluts which, in turn, have
caused a consumer revolt, and declining TV audiences. In Britain, meanwhile,
competitive pressures across the media industries have led to de-layering and
re-structuring, involving a decline in the numbers of journalists and producers—a process that has sometimes been masked by the use of casual labour.[4]

Of course, new technology permits the smaller number of journalists who
remain to be more productive. Yet what is journalistic 'productivity' in the
new market place? On the one hand, armchair journalism has its limitations;
on the other, the decline in the public appetite for news imposes its own. A
recent conference on the civil service and the media brought out other points:
one eminent social affairs correspondent pointed out that the man in Wapping
with too many stories to write is less likely to leave his office, and more likely
to rely on official press releases and the sources you can talk to on the phone.
Official handouts are better than they used to be, but—as a senior civil servant
indicated wearily at the same event—at a time when very few journalists
seemed to understand or want this kind of material any more.

These pressures in turn affect recruitment to journalism, and journalistic
values. The latter appear to be different in Britain from elsewhere. Thus, a
recent survey of British journalists suggested that 47 per cent of them are
prepared to claim to belong to some other profession, in the interests of
getting a story (comparable figure for the US, Australia and Holland were
20 per cent, 13 per cent and 4 per cent respectively) while 65 per cent would be
prepared to pay for information (against 20 per cent, 21 per cent and 20 per
cent). The same survey showed that (in striking contrast to the message given
by media owners to the Calcutt committee), an overwhelming majority of
British journalists (nearly 80 per cent) believed that there should be some legal
constraints on press intrusion into privacy.[5]

Fashionable contemporary theorists claim that all the old problems about
the distribution of access to the media for putting your message across are
simply being resolved in a new way. In the past (so it has been argued), the
problem was one of scarcity: not everyone could set up their own newspaper

or broadcasting station, so disputes about control of the media were really concerned with the allocation of scarce resources. However—according to the conventional wisdom, as expressed in many social science texts, from the works of Anthony Giddens to GCSE sociology primers—'scarcity' in this field is yesterday's crisis, overtaken by modern technology. It is argued that the vast number of stations made available by cable, along with other innovations, have opened up new forms of democratic interactivity, from cyber-cities to wired, responsive town halls. As a result, a multiplicity of channels will dissolve the old problems of allocating the right to speak that was a product of scarcity.

Unfortunately, much of this is speculative at best, if not simply utopian. As yet, scarcity has by no means disappeared: there has merely been a shift in the things that are scarce. Though there are more channels, there has been a shrinkage in the resources available for running them. Indeed, the support services required to supply the information and culture that could provide the super-structure for exciting interactive services is everywhere in crisis. Libraries are underfunded, universities desperately squeezed, cultural activities impoverished.

Musical performance, for example, might have been expected to flourish in a world of proliferating outlets. Actually, the opposite is the case. The British public goes to fewer classical concerts than in the past, the careers of serious musicians have become more precarious and punishing, while major orchestras stagger from one funding catastrophe to the next, and their repertoires get narrower. Yet interest in music has increased: part of the explanation is that it has become a solitary pursuit. Instead of attending performances, music-lovers listen to more classical CDs and tapes than ever before. A related pattern is to be seen in the production of serious news, where the scarcity of support and backup is especially apparent. There is more news, available in more places, than ever in history. News gets to us faster, sometimes in 'real time' as it is actually unfolding. This, in turn, influences the political impact of the news. But news values, what stories run, what and who they should be about, have been remorselessly affected by competitive pressures. Important stories die faster, shunted aside by trivial but consumer-friendly ones.[6]

The job of assessing what should be reported, and what ignored, is made no easier by the large number of channels all eager not to be left behind in the race to be part of the mainstream. There is still scarcity of talented journalists and opportunities to look at unusual problems in a quizzical way: that is something technology has certainly not abolished. The sceptical observer may also conclude that the frequently heard claim that technology 'requires' this or that policy, is often just a way of masking a vested interest in the handy disguise of modernity.

Mill

The observer may also note something else. The main importance of all the swirling commercial and political pressures is their impact, not on the commercial market-place as such, but on the formation of public opinion: how it is shaped, and how it may express itself.

The US First Amendment, and the writings of John Stuart Mill, have long been seen as sacred texts in this debate. In recent years, neo-liberal arguments derived from interpretations of them have become more and more important, governing thought and policy about the media. Ideas, it is suggested, can only be protected if they are, indeed, regarded as artefacts, manufactured goods that may be bought and sold, and whose exchange is best governed by the neutral process of the market. If people like an idea they will buy it. If they buy it, then that means it must be useful to them. Since the market, it is asserted, will always be furnished with novelty ideas—good and bad—so all opinions will be served, and democracy will flourish. All that needs to happen, therefore, is that the forum be kept free and open, and that there should be no tampering with a free press.

There is a pleasing simplicity about such an approach: but the devil is in the detail. In fact, the market in ideas is no freer than the market in motor cars. Take, for example, the EU's work on determining the conditions under which the technological convergence of telecommunications and broadcasting services should take place. Here, the 'free market in ideas' approach is largely irrelevant to what most people would regard as important. When telecommunications involve political and socially produced material (as in broadcasting), and not just private exchanges, there is a justified public concern that standards should be regulated and protected for the sake of democratic objectives. Yet the EU paper (if unamended) is likely to submit 'broadcasting' kinds of content to 'telecommunication' kinds of regulation. The result will be an eclipsing of voices and a diminishing of the conditions of democratic debate.

So although there is no problem with the assertion that ideas need some kind of free market place if they are to flourish, it is also worth considering whether modern interpreters of the classical authorities correctly assess the relevance of the hallowed texts. As always, people find meanings that may not have been intended, or were intended in different circumstances. Thus, it is clear that Mill wanted the quality of political debate to be improved, partly because it made things livelier for those who enjoyed an argument, as well as for the more conventional reason that democratic institutions depended on it; and partly in order to encourage the emergence of new ideas which were necessary to reflect a changing reality.

However, Mill by no means sees the market as the only means of protecting the liberty and vigour of debate, and nor should we. In order to direct attention at the other conditions sustaining a democratic environment for ideas, attention needs to be directed away from the usual concern to protect the rights of speakers, however important these are. It is necessary, as well, to consider, alongside their rights, their *obligations*, and in particular the duty of those with powerful voices and powerful positions in society to exercise responsibility over their right to speak. As we have seen, it is now frequently suggested that we do not have to worry any more about the responsibilities of the right to speak, because everyone will soon be able to be their own 'speaker'. But even if this were to be more evident than it is, the existence of two quite separate conditions for democratic debate should make anxiety about the obligations of speakers legitimate.

Popular music

The first condition is that competing voices should be independent of each other. In fact, however, it has become more and more the case that individual voices—and the outlets through which they are expressed—across the entire terrain of expression are owned, controlled, orchestrated by fewer, larger, companies. Ownership by itself may not be a persistent problem: proprietors may be more concerned with balance sheets than political content. But it does have specific effects at specific times, as, for example, when a new editor or controller is being chosen. The second condition is that voices should reflect varying economic conditions and circumstances. Again, a single conglomerate, owning—say—the *Independent* and the *Mirror* may boast or protest a diversity both of audience and of opinion. Yet, not only are the outlets it controls willy-nilly subject to the same economic pressures as the conglomerate as a whole, the experience of one conglomerate is likely to be similar to that of another at any given time, and reactions to global pressures will be similar. In other words, diversity is likely to be a sham, and similar, bureaucratised solutions will be applied across the board.

In addition, there is the linked problem of novelty. How can we secure new modes of thought, and new approaches to changing conditions? In this respect, the market is surely the reverse of perfect. For example, the television market, *particularly* under conditions of fierce competition, is inclined to favour repeats and old-and-tried formulae rather than new initiatives. In many industries, there is constant pressure to innovate: television is certainly not one of them, and it requires external incentives if it is to do so. When it is stimulated to innovate it is often more commercially successful, in the long term: but there have seldom been moments when commercial pressures, in themselves, produced the advance. Thus, in this case, regulation appears to make the market work better.[7] It is also worth noting that at the moment different media industries have different strategies towards the nurture of novelty. For example, the popular music industry attempts to discover changing tastes by investing in them; publishing, on the other hand, is far less prepared to back what is new and unproven.

The sterility of an approach to the media and media freedom based solely on 'rights' is demonstrated by the debate over the First Amendment. This has recently been interpreted, variously, as sanctioning limitless expenditure on political propaganda; as according to corporations the same rights of free speech as an individual citizen; and as providing no prohibition whatsoever of any kind of expression (even where this is a direct incitement to racial violence).[8] The same debate, based on 'rights', has contributed to the strait-jacket of 'politically correct' writing and speech. Mainly, it has been used to legitimise and enhance the opportunities for money-backed 'freedom' to be exercised, without any attempt either to balance this by promoting expression by the poor, or indeed by defining such freedom in terms that guard the public interest.

If this is a modern interpretation of the classical advocacy of liberty, it is certainly a convoluted one, and arguably a downright distortion. Indeed, Mill was less concerned about the need for legal than for political protection of freedom of speech. 'Protection against the tyranny of the magistrate is not enough', he wrote in *On Liberty*: there was also, as important, a need for protection against the tyranny of prevailing fashion, 'against the tendency of society to impose by other means than civil penalties its own ideas and practices as rules of conduct on those who dissent from them'. In short, Mill was much more worried by conformist public opinion, formed outside the remit of courts of law, than by any legal constraints to freedom.

Indeed, in many ways the most stimulating aspect of Mill's essays is contained in his starkly realistic attitude to public opinion. He makes clear his sense of the danger it embodies: that strongly-held majoritarian views expect and require minority compliance; that the 'tasting' of freedom of expression does not necessarily turn a citizen into a defender of it; and indeed, that the most characteristic feature of public opinion is its intolerance. He points out, tellingly, that most people find real toleration of uncomfortable minority views very disagreeable. He indicates, in sum, that the only way public opinion can be made less monolithic is by improving the scope for genuine argument.

He puts forward four reasons why even those who are confident of their own opinions should encourage a climate in which they can be challenged by argument. He is not, in this passage, concerned with rights or freedom *per se* but with what amounts to an aesthetic or even a romantic view of the process of opinion formation. Argument is necessary, he maintains, as the only way of checking against the possibility of error or, if there is error, correcting it. We need argument, he goes on, because most opinions are neither totally true nor wholly false, and disputation is likely to bring about the best of both, producing a superior view. At the same time, argument is a good way of putting a sound opinion on display, and demonstrating its soundness. Finally, he suggests—humanistically—that people benefit from argument in that it animates their sense of the importance of the ownership of a particular idea.

Jungle

In none of this is there much concern about the sacredness of the 'right' of the oppositional speaker. Indeed, while much political and philosophical atten-tion has been devoted to the fundamental point in Mill's work that the damage done by repressing argument is likely to be greater than most of the harms of offence that people may have to suffer if argument is to be given its head, far less note has been made of Mill's comments on the actual effects of disputation.

Mill does not claim that arguments are born fully-formed, like Athena emerging, already armoured, from the brow of Zeus. He sees them, on the contrary, as helpfully developing in the cut and thrust of debate, with a public audience playing a critical part in the process of correcting and shaping them. 'Very few facts', he claims, 'are able to tell their own story without comments to bring out their meaning'. The impression given is not of a so-called 'neo-liberal' free-market view of the battle of ideas, in which the right of expression is sacrosanct, and the best idea is 'bought' and therefore triumphs. Instead of a Darwinian jungle, he sees the argument-market as a kind of cauldron, in which ideas of varying strength and merit are adapted and fuse.

Mill is no absolute defender of liberty of speech, or of anything else. He is clear that there are some things people cannot be allowed to do, even if they themselves are the only ones involved. A man cannot, for example, decide to abrogate his freedom by selling himself into slavery. Thus, in *Considerations on Representative Government*, he wrote, 'The principle of freedom cannot require that he should not be free'. Extending from Mill to the current debate on the media, it might be maintained (using similar reasoning) that some contemporary things are irreducible, and not available for disposal in the name of a spurious 'purity of freedom' principle. One such thing is press variety and choice. If we stress Mill's concept of 'obligation' as a basis for freedom, rather than arid 'rights', then it could appear that there is an obligation—regardless of the so-called 'rights' of corporate empires—to protect a climate in which genuine argument can flourish.

It is important to note, in particular, that Mill gives primacy, in his case, to the fallibility and corrigibility of public opinion. It is an optimistic doctrine: people can be stupid, stubborn and perverse but, through open debate, they have the capacity to learn, and must be helped to do so. Mill does not see arguments as competing products. On the contrary: he sees them as a fertile brew. He treasures their texture, enjoys their spontaneity whether they are right or wrong, praises the passion with which they are advanced.

He specifically rejects the naive Miltonian view that doctrines were either right or wrong, and men had simply to decide between them. Milton, indeed, was the real precursor of the 1980s right-wing think tank. 'Though all the winds of doctrine are let loose upon the earth,' he wrote, characteristically, '. . . whoever knew truth put to the worse in a free and open encounter? . . . Truth must always prevail in a fair fight with falsehood.' Mill lacked the poet's seventeenth century puritan confidence: or, alternatively, he had a rationalist confidence that exceeded it. For him, 'truth' was something that did not triumph: it emerged, provided the conditions for discussion were right, and this required the nurturing, and education, of public opinion.

According to Mill, concentrating on the preservation of freedom-from-restriction was not bound to produce the best results: what mattered most was not the right to speak, but the obligation to ensure that others were heard. A related point has recently been explored by Onora O'Neil who has argued powerfully that the rights of any individual require, precisely, reciprocal obligations. 'Unfortunately, much writing and rhetoric on rights heedlessly proclaims universal rights', she points out, '. . . without showing what connects each presumed right holder to some specified obligation bearer— which leaves the content of these supposed rights wholly obscure'.[9] As US experience indicates, rights to free speech simply do not, on their own, ensure that vivid and vigorous argument of the kind healthy democracy requires takes place. What such rights do do, of course, is to provide scope for a few, over-mighty voices to dominate any debate; what they do not do is to encourage divergent and novel opinions.

Public service

Thus we are left with a democratic shortfall. If non-interference, unbuttressed, tends to produce political conformity and does not foster fertile debate, then those who are concerned for democracy cannot remain passive. The situation requires a re-examination of the way the concept of obligation is discussed and, in this case, applied. In fact, the idea of obligation is not new to discussion of the role of the media. In British broadcasting, in particular, it has long been fundamental, though recently weakening: it has gone under the label 'public service'. Is there a case for re-considering this idea, as a democratically required obligation?

As we have seen, modern news has merged with entertainment. Yet should we still consider how this particular form of entertainment, and how the 'news' content of other programmes which do not seek to be anything other than entertainment, should address its huge if largely silent audience?[10] There remain many questions: for example, over the difference between so-called political 'balance' (a long-established, and precious, principle in British broadcasting) and objectivity. New questions are raised, too, by public utility regulation. Obligation, however, requires more than the occasional interventions of a regulator.

There is a need to provide a forum to consider such issues and, above all, to develop a view of audiences and readerships that holds them to be active and engaged, not passive and purely consuming. However, Mill put the difficulties well, a century and a half ago in his *Essays on Civilisation*:

There has been much complaint of late years of the growth, both in the world of trade and in that of the intellect, of quackery, and especially of puffing; but nobody seems to have remarked that these are the inevitable fruits of immense competition; of a state of society where any voice not pitched in an exaggerated key is lost in the hubbub. Success in so crowded a field depends not on what a person is, but what he seems; marketable qualities become the object instead of substantial ones, and a man's labour and capital are expended less in doing anything than in persuading other people that he had done it.

Biographical Note

Jean Seaton is Reader in Communications and Quentin Hogg Research Fellow at the University of Westminster. She has written widely on politics and the media.

Notes

1 R. Putnam, 'Bowling Alone: America's declining social capital', *Journal of Democracy*, Jan. 1995.
2 See C. Seymour-Ure, *The British Press and Broadcasting since 1945*, 2nd ed., Oxford, Blackwell, 1996, especially Chapter 5.
3 'Advertising in Markets in the UK and Europe: No Single Market Yet'. EU paper No. 175.
4 ESRC sponsored conference, 'The Civil Service and the Media', 17 March 1996.
5 J. Hemingham, *The News Breed: British Journalists in the 1990s*, London Institute, 1995.
6 N. Gowing, 'Real Time Television: Broadcasting and War'. Shorenstein Centre for Politics and Communication, Kennedy School of Government, Harvard, 1993.
7 The clearest and most surprising exposition of this is to be found in the Peacock Committee report on BBC finances (Cmnd 3270, 1986).
8 For further reading about recent judgments, see J. Lichtenburg, *Democracy and the Mass Media*, Cambridge, CUP, 1993; and D. Allen, ed., *The First Amendment*, Oxford, OUP, 1996.
9 O. O'Neil, *Towards Justice and Virtue*, Cambridge, CUP, 1996, p. 132.
10 See P. Scannell, *Broadcasting and Modernity*, Oxford, Blackwell, 1997, which is concerned with the way in which broadcasters learnt to address the public in the light of their perceived obligations towards it.

Index

accountability 52
Acland, E. 92
advertising 36, 85, 122
Ahmed, A. 84
Altrincham, Lord 99–100
Anderson, B. 55
Annan Committee 109–10
Arledge, R. 77
Astor of Hever, Lord 45
Attlee, C. 10

Bacharach, M. 34–5
Bagehot, W. 92, 102
Baldwin, S. 52
Baltimore Sun 99
Barnett, A. 59
'Barnett formula' 71
Barrie, J. M. 93
BBC (British Broadcasting Corporation)
    and Royal Family 100, 105
BBC Radio Scotland 66–7
BBC Television Scotland 66, 67–8
Beaton, C. 97, 99
Beaverbrook, Lord 45, 52
Beckett, M. 45
Bell, M. 88–9
Berlin, I. 36
Berlusconi, S. 50
Bertelsmann Foundation 39
Biggam, R. 67
Billig, M. 55
Black, C. 45
Blair, T. 8, 10, 11, 16, 58, 108
Blumler, J. 25
Boothroyd, B. 8
Border Television 64
Boston Globe 103
Brabourne, Lord 101
Bragg, M. 39
Branson, R. 50
British National Party 114
Britishness 56
Brittan, S. 38
Broadcasting Act 1990 110, 111, 114–15

Broadcasting for Scotland Campaign 65,
    68
broadcasting policy 37–42
Broadcasting Standards Commission 112
broadcasting studios
    arenas of debate 8, 9–10
Brown, G. 10, 10–11
BSE (Bovine Spongiform Encephalo-
    pathy) crisis 28, 57, 112
BSkyB 36

Calcutt Committee on Privacy 88, 122
Caledonian Newspapers 63
Campbell, A. 15, 16
Cawston, R. 101
Channel 4 69, 83–4
Charles, Prince of Wales 101–3, 105
Chichester, F. 48, 101
children's programmes 77
Churchill, W. 10, 96
civic role of media 20–1, 23, 25–6
Clarke, K. 11
Clinton, B. 78, 86
College Green 117–18
Columbia University School of
    Journalism 76
columnists 44
Colville, R. 97
communications directors 10
community 36
competition 82–3, 123
Conditional Access Systems (CAS) 33–4
conglomerates 46, 63–6, 125
consumer choice 34–5, 84, 121
Cosgrove, S. 69
Courier 63
courts of law 111–12, 113, 113–16
Crawford, M. 96–7
critical journalism 79
Curran, J. 85
current affairs programmes 80–1

Daily Express 101
Daily Herald 49

Published by Blackwell Publishers, 108 Cowley Road, Oxford OX4 1JF, UK and 350 Main Street, Malden, MA 02148, USA

DATE DUE

HIGHSMITH #45115